# People

Alan Bennett has been one of our leading dramatists since the success of *Beyond the Fringe* in the 1960s. His television series *Talking Heads* has become a modern-day classic, as have many of his works for stage including *Forty Years On*, *The Lady in the Van*, *A Question of Attribution*, *The Madness of George III* (together with the Oscar-nominated screenplay *The Madness of King George*) and an adaptation of Kenneth Grahame's *The Wind in the Willows*. At the National Theatre, London, *The History Boys* won numerous awards including *Evening Standard* and Critics' Circle awards for Best Play, an Olivier for Best New Play and the South Bank Award. On Broadway, *The History Boys* won five New York Drama Desk Awards, four Outer Critics' Circle Awards, a New York Drama Critics' Award, a New York Drama League Award and six Tonys. His collection of prose, *Untold Stories*, won the PEN/Ackerley Prize for autobiography, 2006. *The Uncommon Reader* was published in 2007 and *Smut: Two Unseemly Stories* in 2011.

ALAN BENNETT

# People

*with an introduction by the author*

*faber and faber*

First published in 2012
by Faber and Faber Limited
74–77 Great Russell Street
London WC1B 3DA

Typeset by Country Setting, Kingsdown, Kent CT14 8ES
Printed and bound by CPI Group (UK) Ltd, Croydon, CR0 4YY

A CIP record for this book is available from the British Library

ISBN
978-0-571-29688-0 (hbk)
978-0-571-129689-7 (pbk)

2 4 6 8 10 9 7 5 3 1

# Introduction

I sometimes think that my plays are just an excuse for the introductions with which they are generally accompanied. These preambles, while often gossipy and with sidelights on the rehearsal process, also provide me with a soapbox from which I can address, sometimes more directly than I've managed in the play itself, some of the themes that crop up in the text. In *The History Boys* it was private education; in *The Habit of Art* biography; in *People*, though, I'm not sure.

Rehearsals aren't just for the actors; they are also a first opportunity for the author to hear the play and find out what he or she has written. But since this introduction is being put together in August 2012, nearly two months before rehearsals begin, I am still to some extent in the dark about the play or what (if anything) it adds up to.

Some plays seem to start with an itch, an irritation, something one can't solve or a feeling one can't locate. With *People* it was a sense of unease when going round a National Trust house and being required to buy into the role of reverential visitor. I knew this irritated me, but, like the hapless visitors whom Dorothy confronts as they are leaving, I still found it hard to say what it was I had expected to find and whether I had found it.

National Trust guides more conventional than Dorothy (and for whom I almost invariably feel slightly sorry) assume that one wishes to be informed about the room or its furniture and pictures, which I don't always. Sometimes I just want to look and occasionally (eighteenth-century porcelain, Chinoiserie and most tapestries) prefer to walk straight through. Sometimes I actively dislike what I'm seeing: yet another table massively laid for a banquet, for instance, or massed ranks of the family photos ranged on top of a grand piano with royal visitors given some prominence. Even when I am interested but want to be left alone with the pictures or whatever, I have learned not to show too much interest as this invariably fetches the guide over, wanting to share his or her expertise. I know this is bad behaviour and it's another reason why I'll often come away as dissatisfied with myself as I am with the house.

The first stately home I can remember visiting was Temple Newsam, a handsome early sixteenth-century house given to Leeds by the earl of Halifax. We often used to go on outings there when I was a child, taking the tram from outside the City Market up through Halton and past the municipal golf course to the terminus at Temple Newsam House. An adjunct of Leeds Art Gallery, it had a good collection of furniture, a long gallery without which no country house was complete, besides housing some of the city's collection of Cotman drawings and watercolours. While aged nine or ten I didn't wholly appreciate its contents, I saw Temple Newsam as a wonderfully ancient and romantic place, which it wasn't really, having been heavily restored and remodelled in the nineteenth century. Still, it gave me a lifelong taste for enfiladed rooms and for Leeds pottery (particularly the horses) neither of which life has enabled me to indulge. As a boy, though, for me its most numinous holding was a large felt hat reputed to be that of Oliver Cromwell with a bullet hole in the crown to prove it.

Visiting Temple Newsam was always a treat, as it still is more than half a century later. Back in 1947, though, with the country in the throes of the post-war economic crisis, the push was on for more coal, and the whole of the park in front of the house was given over to open-cast mining, the excavations for which came right up to the terrace. From the state rooms you looked out on a landscape as bleak and blasted as a view of the Somme, an idyll, as it seemed to me then, irretrievably lost, and young though I was I knew this.

But of course I was wrong. It wasn't irretrievable and to look at the grounds today one would have no idea that such a violation had ever occurred. And it had occurred, too, with even greater devastation at other country houses south of Leeds: Nostell Priory was similarly beleaguered, as was Wentworth Woodhouse, both, like the Stacpooles' house, smack in the middle of coal-bearing country and where the notion as in the play of a country house with a mine in the immediate vicinity is far from far-fetched.

Nostell Priory is full of Adam furniture, and both Nostell and Temple Newsam have Chippendale desks like the one referred to in the play, that at Temple Newsam, bought by Leeds Corporation from the Harewoods at Harewood House – another outing from Leeds, and a mansion, incidentally, that was once on the National Trust's wish list but which happily still remains with the family that built it. It is, though, one of those reprobate mansions cited by June in the play, Harewood having been built from the profits of eighteenth-century sugar and slaves . . . from one of whom is descended one of the National Theatre's noted actors, David Harewood.

Previous productions of my plays at the National Theatre have generally been accompanied by a Platform evening, very often shared with Nicholas Hytner, when we talk about the play and answer questions from the audience. We did one of these evenings in 2009 after the opening of *The Habit of Art*, and at the end of the session Nick thanked the audience, saying that my plays seemed to turn up (and be put through his letter box) at roughly four-year intervals. He felt this was a bit long to wait and if the audience agreed and wanted something sooner he asked them to put their hands together. This they gratifyingly did. It was a Tinkerbell moment, and not having known what he was planning to say I found myself uncharacteristically choked up. But it did the trick, this play clocking in at three years after its predecessor.

When I first showed it to Nick he remarked that it wasn't like anything else I'd done . . . or anything else I'd done with him. The play, though, that does have hints of it is *Getting On* (1971), which, like *People*, is what has since become known as a 'play for England', sort of, anyway. In those days when I had less compassion for the audience (and for the actors) I went in for much longer speeches than I would venture to do nowadays. But some of the diatribes I put into the mouth of George Oliver, a right-wing Labour MP, are echoes of the complaints more succinctly expressed by Dorothy in *People*, the complaints generally being about 'England'.

*Enjoy* (1980) is another play with which *People* has similarities in that both, while ostensibly contemporary in setting, have a slightly fanciful notion of the future. At least I thought of it as fanciful, but what I was writing about in *Enjoy* – the decay and preservation of a working-class quarter in a northern town and the last back-to-back in Leeds – all came true much quicker than I could have imagined in the decades that followed. The same threatens to be the case with *People*.

Privacy or at any rate exclusivity is increasingly for hire, instances of which make some of Bevan's proposals in the play not even outlandish. I had written the play when I read that Lichtenstein in its entirety could be hired for the relatively modest sum of £40,000 per night. Around the same time I read that Lancaster Castle, that once housed the County Court and the prison that often went with such institutions, was up for sale. That it had also hosted the execution of condemned prisoners probably increased the estimate. At one point in 2011 the Merchant Navy War Memorial at Tower Hill was to have been hired out for some banker's junket. That a Methodist church in Bourne-mouth has been bought and re-opened as a Tesco is hardly worth mentioning. So what is? Everywhere nowadays has its price and the more inappropriate the setting the better. I scarcely dare suggest that Pentonville or Wormwood Scrubs be marketed as fun venues lest it has already happened.

When it came to giving offence, there too I kept finding that I had been if not timid, at least over-scrupulous. In the management and presentation of their newly acquired property of Stacpole House I imagined the Trust as entirely without inhibition, ready to exploit any aspect of the property's recent history to draw in the public, wholly unembarrassed by the seedy or the disreputable. I envisaged a series of events I took to be wildly implausible, but in the light of recent developments they turn out to be almost tame.

I read for instance that the audio guide to the National Trust house at Hughenden, once lived in by Disraeli, is voiced by Jeffrey Archer, euphemistically described by the Trust as 'a provocative figure'. And in the matter of pornography the Trust has recently sponsored a tape to accompany a tour round London's Soho, the highlights of which are not architectural. It is apparently selling very well.

My objections to this level of marketing are not to do with morals but to do with taste. In another connection, though, and nothing to do with the Trust, I found life had outstripped my paltry imagination. I have no reference for this other than what the DNB used to call 'personal knowledge', but talking to someone about what I still thought of as the outrageousness of a country house being made the venue for a porn film, I was told that there was (and maybe still is) an entrepreneur who does just that, arranging similar (and equally chilly) filming in country houses north of the border.

So, writing the play and imagining I was ahead of my times, I then found I was scarcely even abreast of them. Had the play not been produced when it was (in November

2012), in six months' time it might have seemed hopelessly out of date.

As is made plain in the play, Dorothy is not shocked by porn being filmed under her (leaking) roof. As she points out, she is a peeress in her own right. 'The middle class . . . they're the respectable ones.' Which is a cliché but I'd have thought no less true for all that. But then, what do I know?

My experience of high life is limited, but years ago, I think through George Melly, I used to be invited to parties given by Geoffrey Bennison, the fashionable interior decorator. He lived in Golden Square ('Above Glorex Woollens, dear') and there one would find Geoffrey in full drag, and very convincing drag it was, too, as he made no attempt to seem glamorous, instead coming across as a middle-aged duchess not unlike Lady Montdore in Nancy Mitford's *Love in a Cold Climate*. It would be a very mixed bag of high life and low life – Diana Duff Cooper dancing with a well-known burglar sticks in the mind – respectability and the middle classes nowhere.

'Now that I'm eighty there are two things I no longer have to do,' said another grand lady of my acquaintance. 'Tell the truth and wear knickers.' What Dorothy is or is not wearing under her fur coat I don't like to think.

That said, I have never been entirely confident that the glimpses one is allowed in stately homes of the family's 'real life' always ring true. Years ago I was filming at Penshurst Place, the home of Lord de Lisle and Dudley, and I wrote in my diary (15 December 1984):

The house is everything one imagines an English country house should be . . . a hotchpotch of different periods – mediaeval hall, eighteenth-century courtyards, Gothick front, solid green walls of yew and parterres of box. We film in a gallery adjoining the drawing room, part of the private wing, with photographs of Lord D. at

Cambridge, in India as a young man and ADC to Wavell and now standing beside Macmillan as he unveils a plaque to Lord Gort. On a coffee table are back numbers of *The Economist*, *Country Life* and the *TLS* with drinks on the side.

'Ah,' one thinks. 'A glimpse here of the private life.' But is it? Is this really a private room or just a private room for public consumption? These drinks (and the bottle of vitamin pills beside them), have they been artfully arranged to suggest a private life? Is there somewhere else, another flat which is *more* private? And so on. And so on. The impression is confirmed by the hall table, on which are all the Viscount's hats: his green Guards trilbies, his bowler, his lumberjack's hat that was plainly presented to him on some sort of ceremonial visit. Surely, all this is meant to be *seen*?

(*Writing Home*)

No soiled underwear in the state bedroom at least . . . but even voicing the thought I can see it coming one day soon. The links between such unworthy musings and what happens in the play are obvious.

Plays have buds, points at which something is mentioned in one play though not dwelt on but which turns up in a later play. Never sure of the significance of what one writes or the continuity of one's concerns, I find these recurrences reassuring as pointing if nothing else to consistency. They can, though, be shaming.

In *The History Boys* Irwin is a dynamic supply teacher who ends up as a TV historian and government special adviser. Televised in the latrine passage below the reredorter at Rievaulx Abbey, he speculates on those scraps of cloth on which the monks wiped their bums, some of which have been recovered and are in the abbey museum. Could it be shown that one of these fragments had actually been used by St Aelred of Rievaulx, would that scrap of cloth,

Irwin wonders, then constitute a sacred relic? It's an unsavoury preoccupation, but unnoticed by me a related concept has smuggled itself into *People*, where the notion of historical and celebrity urine is a branch grown from Irwin's bud.

On a different level the discussion of the Holocaust in *The History Boys* relates to Hector's dismay that Auschwitz has become just another station on the tourist trail, with Hector concerned about the proportion of reverence to prurience among the visitors. This recurs – and to my mind more harshly – in *People*, with Lumsden's comment that there is 'nowhere that is not visitable. That at least the Holocaust has taught us.'

Dorothy's comments about the graffiti done by the Canadian troops billeted in the house during the war echo similar speculations in James Lees-Milne's *Ancestral Voices:*

WEDNESDAY 7 JANUARY 1942 (At Brocket) I walked across a stile and down a footpath to the James Paine bridge, which the Canadian troops have disfigured by cutting their names, with addresses in Canada, and personal numbers, all complete and inches deep – the vandals. Yet, I thought, what an interesting memorial this will be in years to come and quite traditional, like the German mercenaries' names scrawled in 1530 on the Palazzo Ducale in Urbino.

He might have added the Viking inscriptions cut centuries earlier into the lions outside the Arsenale in Venice.

It was in Lees-Milne, too, that I read about the Jungmann sisters, who in their youth were Bright Young Things and contemporaries of Evelyn Waugh. In later life they turned reclusive, stockpiled the newspaper (the *Telegraph*, I suspect), reading one a day still but years behind the times.

It has been said (by Kathryn Hughes in the *Guardian*) that nowadays 'it is the demotic and the diurnal that matter to us when thinking about the past' and what are generally called 'bygones' make a brief appearance in the play, as they regularly do in the below-stairs rooms of country houses. Fortunate in having had a relatively long life, I have grown used to seeing everyday items from my childhood featuring in folk museums or even as items on the *Antiques Road Show*, a brass and pewter gill measure from a milk pail, for instance (wielded at the Bennett family back door by the milkman, Mr Keen, his horse and trap waiting in the street); a posser for the clothes wash and jelly moulds galore.

Even so I was surprised this summer when going round Blickling to see a young man rapt in contemplation of a perfectly ordinary aluminium pan. Still, he was doubtless a dab hand at the computer, which I'm not, even though to me aluminium pans are commonplace. Other vintage items which were in common use when I was young would be:

A wicker carpet beater.
A wooden clothes horse.
A tidy betty.
A flat iron. ,
Pottery eggs.
Spats.
Black lead.
Virol.

The danger of making such a list is that one will in due course figure on it.

Curiously it was only when I'd finished the play that I realised I'd managed to avoid giving the house a name. I suppose it ought to be the family name and so Stacpoole, except that one proof of aristocracy is to subtly distinguish the name of the house from the name of its location. Thus in a minor snobbery Harewood, the home of the Lascelles family and their earldom, is pronounced Harwood, whereas the village of Harewood, its location near Leeds, is pronounced as it's spelled, Hare-wood. So on a similar principle I've called the house Stacpole but it's pronounced Stacpool.

In the play Bevan sings the praises of solitude with his slogan 'P-S-T . . . people spoil things.' While Bevan hardly carries the moral burden of the play he has a point . . . and some authorial sympathy.

I have tasted the pleasures of singularity myself, having been lucky enough to be in Westminster Abbey at midnight and virtually alone. As an ex-trustee I am permitted to visit the National Gallery after hours, and filming has meant that I have often been in well-loved places like Fountains Abbey almost on my own.

So, while it is to be hoped that such privileged privacies are never marketed in the way Bevan and 'The Concern' would like, the heady delights of exclusion are these days touted commercially more and more and without apology.

The notion that the eighties in England marked a turning point keeps recurring – a time when, as Dorothy is told, we ceased to take things for granted and self-interest and self-servingness took over. Some of this alteration in public life can be put down to the pushing back of the boundaries of the state as begun under Mrs Thatcher and pursued even more disastrously thereafter, though in regretting this (and not being able to be more specific about it) Dorothy in her fur coat and gym shoes is thought by her sister the archdeacon to be pitiably naive as perhaps I am, who feels much the same. The state has never frightened me. Why should it? It gave me my education (and in those days it was a gift); it saved my father's life as it has on occasion saved mine by services we are now told have to be paid for.

What is harder to put one's finger on is the growth of surliness in public behaviour and the sour taste of public life. There has been a diminution of magnanimity in government both central and local, with the public finding itself re-branded as 'customers', supposedly to dignify our require-ments but in effect to make us available for easier exploitation. The faith – which like most ideologies has only a tangential connection with reason – is that everything must make a profit and that there is nothing that cannot be bought and sold.

These thoughts are so obvious that I hesitate to put them down, still less make them specific in the play. Dorothy is asking what is different about England, saying how she misses things being taken for granted. We were told in the eighties and pretty constantly since that we can't afford to take anything for granted, whereas to my mind in a truly civilised state the more that can be taken for granted in terms of health, education, employment and welfare the better we are for it. Less and less are we a nation and more and more just a captive market to be exploited. 'I hate it,' says Dorothy, and she doesn't just mean showing people round the house.

Apropos the closet with the ancient chamber pots: having finished the play, we went for a short holiday in Norfolk in the course of which we went round Felbrigg Hall, the family home of R. W. Ketton-Cremer, who willed it to the National Trust on his death in 1969. Ketton-Cremer was an historian and had a well-stocked Gothick library which, as distinct from other such rooms in country houses, was a place of work, as Ketton-Cremer produced many books. Set in the thickness of the wall behind a pivoting bookcase was a closet with, on a table, a chamber pot. It was, alas, empty.

I end as I have ended the introductions to the previous five plays on which we've worked together with my heartfelt thanks to Nicholas Hytner. He brings to life what to me on the page often seems dull. I write plays; he turns them into theatre. His productions of the plays are always a pleasure to work on and he emboldens me in writing them. And it's always fun. 'Plays is work,' said Ellen Terry. 'No play about it.' But then she never worked with Nicholas Hytner.

Thanks too to another encourager, Dinah Wood, my editor at Faber, and of course to all the cast of the play and the staff of the National. To turn up every few years with a play and still find oneself welcome is a great pleasure. It has its moments though. When I went in on the first day of rehearsal for *People* someone at the stage door said, 'Still hanging on then?'

**People** was first performed in the Lyttelton auditorium of the National Theatre, London, on 31 October 2012. The cast was as follows:

**Theodore**  Peter Egan
**Dorothy Stacpoole**  Frances de la Tour
**Bevan**  Miles Jupp
**Iris**  Linda Bassett
**June Stacpoole**  Selina Cadell
**Ralph Lumsden**  Nicholas le Prevost
**Bishop**  Andy de la Tour
**Bruce**  Alastair Parker
**Louise**  Frances Ashman
**Nigel**  Giles Cooper
**Les**  Jack Chissick
**Colin**  Robin Pearce
**Brit**  Jess Murphy
**Ensemble**  Ellie Burrow, Philip Childs, Carole Dance, Barbara Kirby, Alexander Warner

*Director*  Nicholas Hytner
*Designer*  Bob Crowley
*Lighting Designer*  James Farncombe
*Music*  George Fenton
*Sound Designer*  Rich Walsh
*Movement Director*  Jonathan Watkins

# Characters

**Dorothy Stacpoole**

**June Stacpoole**

**Iris**

**Bevan**

**Ralph Lumsden**

**The Bishop**

**Mr Theodore**

**Bruce**
grip

**Louise**
wardrobe

**Nigel**
assistant director

**Les**
camera

**Colin**
actor

**Brit**
actress

# PEOPLE

# Act One

*A large room in a shabby country house. There is a suggestion of other rooms leading off it, one with double doors. A bagged chandelier possibly and long windows, shuttered. Through a crack in the double doors a line of very bright light suggests filming of some sort. The whole room is shabby and run down but very grand. It is also cold.*

**Theodore** (*in shadow*) South Yorkshire and a fine rain falling. Keep it together. And action.

*Light grows on two women, both in their seventies, Dorothy, tall and grand in an old fur coat and gym shoes. Iris, more downtrodden, is similarly shabby.*
*Dorothy suddenly stands up and claps her hands.*
*A pause and she does it again. And again.*
*She is catching moths.*
*Suddenly the double doors open briefly with a bright shaft of light from the room beyond. A youngish man comes through, shuts the door carefully and quietly, then crouches down by the door. Maybe he wears a short military-style jacket. Otherwise he is naked.*
*Pause.*

**Dorothy** Are we dangerous?

*Colin (the young man) puts his finger to his lips and with a turning movement of his hand makes the sign indicating that a camera is turning over and filming going on.*
*Dorothy turns to Iris, puts her finger to her lips and makes a similar movement for Iris's benefit, who takes no notice of either of them and is perhaps knitting.*

3

*Dorothy sits down and the three of them are silent.*
*Faintly but distinctly from the room next door come*
*the sounds of creaking bedsprings and possibly the*
*occasional woman's cry.*
*Dorothy has a wide forgiving smile on her face and*
*seems impervious. Iris is impervious to everything.*
*Lights and sounds fade as the upper-class voice of*
*Bevan, a man in his thirties, carries us through into the*
*next scene which is the same minus the shaft of light*
*and the naked man and also minus Dorothy.*

**Bevan** (*possibly dictating into his iPod or whatever*) One
hip bath. Two nursery fireguards. One croquet set,
mallets, hoops and balls included, in its original Army
and Navy Stores box . . . a touching . . . no, a poignant
reminder of the time when the house served as a
convalescent home for officers during the First War.
(Well, it's the right date).
   Is she a recluse, then?

**Iris** Who's she, the cat's mother? We're neither of us
recluses. I go to the shop.

*Bevan goes on dictating (possibly from notes) while*
*Iris talks through regardless.*

**Bevan** A run of seventeenth-century limewood panelling.

**Iris** That's not a recluse.

**Bevan** Some worm.

**Iris** She doesn't, but you can't expect it.

**Bevan** Five leather fire buckets painted with the Stacpoole
arms.

**Iris** You can't have them. They're for the roof.
   Recluse! People come all the time. The gas comes. The
electric. And she plays billiards. Or she did. Only there's
a bath on the billiard table.

4

**Bevan** No problem. One Victorian nursery scrap screen. A rocking horse similarly.

**Iris** And sometimes I have a walk in the park.

**Bevan** How? It's a jungle.

**Iris** Not our park. Over the hill, where the colliery was. They call it a park. A business park. No seats, no flowers. Prefabs they look like. But no muck any more.

**Bevan** Gas masks. Four. Four?

**Iris** Arthur, the noble one who was killed in the war. Henry, the naughty one, and Dorothy.

**Bevan** Why was Henry naughty?

*Pause.*

Drink?

**Iris** And lorry drivers. As a baby he was very wrinkled. The gas mask was an improvement. He was a love.

**Bevan** So that's three. Whose is the other one?

**Iris** Mine.

**Bevan** Now for the prize. A Chippendale bed, in its original wrappings, never unpacked. Unbelievable.

**Iris** Yes. And you can't have it.

**Dorothy** (*coming in*) Iris, leave the young man alone. This isn't a social call.

**Iris** I'm just passing the time of day. Somebody has to.

**Dorothy** Are you nearly done? Who are you talking to?

**Bevan** Nobody. Myself.

**Dorothy** Does it remember?

**Bevan** If I tell it to.

5

**Dorothy** Perhaps I should get one. Only who would I talk to?

**Bevan** It'll find you somebody.

**Dorothy** Really? What if I don't like him?

**Bevan** Then it'll find you someone else. The bed . . .

**Dorothy** No, Iris is right. You can't have the bed. I'm not a fool.

**Bevan** No problem. Now, what else? Sets of skates, two; console table, one, parcel gilt, possibly Kent.

**Iris** It's not Kent. Why do you think it's in the attic?

**Bevan** So who is it?

**Iris** Gibbs more likely.

**Dorothy** Don't look at me. Iris knows.

**Bevan** (*into his iPod*) Query Gibbs.
A title for the sale: 'A Piece of England'.

**Dorothy** A piece of flannel.

**Bevan** One Coronation stool, 1953.

**Dorothy** You can't have that. The Trust may want that.

**Bevan** Are they in the picture?

**Dorothy** My sister thinks so.

**Bevan** And you don't?

*Dorothy ignores this.*

You have issues where the Trust is concerned?

**Dorothy** I don't know what that means.

**Bevan** You'll forgive my asking, but weren't you the model? My mother remembers you. I only mention it because I'm wondering if that could be some sort of tie-in. Do you have any of your old frocks?

6

**Dorothy** Perhaps I do. Perhaps I don't.

**Bevan** Say they were in the attic they could be part of the sale.

**Iris** They are in the attic.

**Bevan** Various receptacles. A coal scuttle . . .

**Dorothy** No buckets.

**Iris** I told him.

**Bevan** Hardly buckets . . . A Wedgwood jardinière. A seventeenth-century close stool . . .

**Dorothy** Buckets. The roof leaks. You're wanting to sell the few things in the house that still have a point.

**Bevan** What would be the endowment?

**Dorothy** What of?

**Bevan** For the Trust. What land are you offering?

**Dorothy** Land?

**Bevan** They don't just accept properties for nothing. Cash or land, you have to pay them.

**Dorothy** One has to pay them in order to make a gift? That's outrageous. Will my sister know this?

**Iris** She'll know. She's a vicar. She'll have kept it to herself.

**Bevan** You'd be better advised to sell the house outright and then dispose of the contents separately.

**Dorothy** Through you, of course.

**Bevan** We could handle it, certainly.

**Dorothy** My sister wouldn't approve. She keeps harping on about death duties.

**Bevan** The only people who pay death duties, Lady Dorothy, are those who have been too lazy to avoid them. Income tax similarly.

**Dorothy** My sister thinks the house and its contents should be kept together.

**Bevan** Ye–es. Though I personally think that's rather selfish. Release all your wonderful treasures on to the open market and they are there for everyone to enjoy. It's a kind of emancipation, a setting them free to range the world . . . a saleroom here, an exhibition there; art, Lady Stacpoole, is a rover.

*Pause.*

The Adam furniture would break all records. The Chippendale desk is priceless.

**Dorothy** Possibly, but what one truly wants is an en-suite bathroom. I long to be warm at night and be able to undress in front of the fire, like I did as a child. Actually these days I'd be happy to undress at all.

**Bevan** To be honest . . .

**Dorothy** To be honest? To be honest? You're an auctioneer.

**Bevan** What I suggest is that we use this attic sale as a toe in the water . . . a hint of more to follow.

**Dorothy** June permitting.

**Bevan** June?

**Iris** The sister. She's an archbishop.

**Dorothy** She's an archdeacon.

**Iris** She's a madam.

**Bevan** I'm sure that did you decide to dispose of some of the grander stuff – the Louis XV bergères, the Adam

8

suite – we could come to some arrangement about the commission.

**Dorothy** Oh, you charge commission too? You're all at it.

**Bevan** We charge the seller something but we charge the buyer more.

**Dorothy** You're worse than the Trust.

**Bevan** So. Don't sell. Gift the house and its contents to a grateful nation and see what thanks you get.

**Dorothy** One doesn't want gratitude. All one wants is a non-arctic bathroom. What I don't want is people traipsing through.

**Bevan** Who does?

**Dorothy** The National Trust.

**Bevan** Exactly. Still, don't get me wrong. Because, hand on heart, truthfully the Trust has no more sincere admirer. As a business model it is enviable.

*He wanders the room, casing the joint, picking up items, looking at them, putting them back.*

All those fervent dishwashers and painstaking cleaners of tapestry, that vast volunteer army doing the job for love, or company, or just to get out of the house. The Trust's actual wage bill must be minute. Those worthy women and occasional men, sitting sentinel in every room . . . and for what? A cup of tea and a flapjack. The Trust has found a way of capitalising on good will: service to the big house. It's the new feudalism.

**Dorothy** One never saw much wrong with the old. All this . . . and we're poor.

**Bevan** Nothing new there. And what I say is, bring it on.

**Dorothy** 'Bring it on'? What does that mean?

**Bevan** Oh . . . let it happen.

9

**Dorothy** Let what happen?

**Bevan** People having to sell up. Move out. It's an opportunity.

**Iris** Not if nobody can afford to buy.

**Bevan** Some people can. Always. And the worse the time, the better they like it. Boom not. Prosperity not. Slump yes.

**Dorothy** What is this 'not'? 'Not'?

**Bevan** It's an expression.

**Dorothy** I'm beginning to think I've had a stroke.

**Bevan** Did you see the Leonardo? The show?

**Dorothy** The last show I saw was the Diaghilev exhibition in . . . 1954.

**Bevan** The Leonardo was torture. People with headphones on, bumping into you, clumsy, smelly, crowded. The art nowhere.

*Pause.*

And there's no need.
    What is the biggest luxury in the world?

**Dorothy** Central heating?

**Bevan** It is having the place to yourself.
    What is the worst thing in the world?
    Other people. P-S-T.

**Dorothy** I'm sorry?

**Bevan** People Spoil Things.
    May I speak in confidence and not wearing my saleroom hat? I also act for a group of philanthropists . . . names would be meaningless . . . let's just call them The Concern. The Concern has unlimited resources . . . truly unlimited . . . and is interested in acquiring holdings and

properties on behalf of its members . . . estates, great houses, moorlands . . . hospitals, of course, libraries . . . islands . . . Anglesey we recently bought, though that isn't generally known, the object of our communities, most of them of course gated, being to impinge on common humanity as little as possible.

**Dorothy** So you're like the National Trust?

**Bevan** Emphatically unlike. The reverse in fact.

**Dorothy** Oh. Not.

**Bevan** The Trust is concerned with people . . . access, in a word, sharing. We ask the question: why should one share? After all, nobody really believes in sharing. We do it if we have to but if one is in the fortunate position of being able to keep things to oneself why share?

**Dorothy** But why would your people – The Concern? – want this house?

**Bevan** At first sight not sharing might seem like selfishness.

**Dorothy** *Mais non!*

**Bevan** It isn't but we need a theory, a philosophy if you like, to explain why. I see this house as a possible study centre for The Concern, a think tank, a seed bed of all that is best in England. Untouched for five centuries, added to but not altered . . . it's an image of our nation. But, no people . . . no other people. Like-minded people, like-moneyed people . . . but as I emphasise again we do not share.

> *There is a noise, something between a creak and a groan somewhere in the depths beneath the house.*

**Bevan** Dear God, what's that?

**Dorothy** (*unalarmed*) The coal.

**Bevan** The coal?

**Dorothy** After the war the park was requisitioned for open-cast mining, came right up to the terrace. They got out all the coal except, obviously, what the house is built on. So we now stand on a pillar of coal – and occasionally it grumbles.

**Bevan** But is it safe?

**Dorothy** Oh yes.
  One isn't going to plummet into the bowels of the earth. They went into all that.

**Bevan** That rather reinforces what I was going to say. Love it as one does, South Yorkshire isn't a must-have location. We would want to move the house.

**Dorothy** Move it?

**Iris** Why? It's very handy for Sheffield.

**Bevan** Picture this house in the cosiness of Dorset, say, or well-bred Wiltshire. Handier, warmer, cleaner.

**Dorothy** Dorset? Wouldn't the planners object?

**Bevan** Dear sweet, charming, innocent lady. No problem. We don't operate at that level. Would you mind if we did that . . . moved you? You could live in the lodge.

**Dorothy** I might. I might not.

**Bevan** What would your objection be?

**Dorothy** Love, Mr Bevan?

**Bevan** Yes. I have heard of it.

**Dorothy** Would they do an en-suite bathroom?

**Iris** Would they do two?

**Bevan** I think you can be assured of that.

*The telephone rings. Iris answers.*

**Iris**  Yes?
  Now?

*She puts the phone down.*

Madam.

**Dorothy**  Already?

**Iris**  You know her.

**Dorothy**  You must go.

**Bevan**  Really?

**Dorothy**  This minute.

**Bevan**  Well, let me quickly write down a ball-park figure that the house and contents might fetch on the open market.

*He shows it to her.*

Whereas this, somewhat larger figure – ball-park again – what the Concern would pay.

**Dorothy**  You would pay more?

**Bevan**  For discretion and a quick sale, yes.

*Dorothy looks at it and shows it to Iris.*

**Iris**  We haven't got a ball park.

**Bevan**  One thing puzzles me. In the attic two or three rooms seem to be full of newspapers just piled up.

**Dorothy**  Yes. I read them.
  At one period in my life I got behind but I now read one a day. I shall catch up.

**Bevan**  How?

**Dorothy**  There's bound to be a strike. Then I shall be laughing.

**Bevan**  This house has been on our wish list from the start so someone else may call, just to look it over. But in any event I will be back next week and we can talk further.

**Dorothy**  Good. Off you go.

*He is going out when he stops.*

**Bevan**  What is this?

*He picks up an unassuming little bowl from the floor.*

**Dorothy**  What does it look like? It's the cat's bowl.

*Bevan looks at it carefully, possibly with a magnifying glass.*

**Bevan**  Does this come with the contents?

**Dorothy**  It could do.

**Iris**  Where does that leave the cat?

**Bevan**  The auction figure I wrote down. Double it.
Put this away. Somewhere safe.

**Dorothy**  You'd better go. We don't want you running into my sister.

**Bevan**  No problem. It might be useful. I could put the proposal to her.

**Dorothy**  There is a problem. I'm the one who decides.

**Bevan**  Goodbye. And remember. P-S-T.

*Iris snorts. He goes.*

**Iris**  Well? What do you think?

**Dorothy**  I was brought up never to trust anyone in a camel-hair coat. Still. No people. I like the sound of that.

*They look at the cat's bowl.*

**Iris**  You don't want to give them your necklace.

**Dorothy** I don't want to *give* them anything.

**Iris** Where is it?

**Dorothy** Upstairs. In a drawer somewhere.

**Iris** Like a lot of things.

**Dorothy** No problem.

*Dorothy picks up the cat's bowl, and the wrapping of it and the putting of it away turns into a song and dance for them both to the tune of 'Downtown' – done out of sheer high spirits because of the value of the bowl. When June calls out they stop, embarrassed.*

**June** (*off*) Hello! Hello!

**Dorothy** Don't let on to June.

**Iris** Me? What about?

**Dorothy** (*mouthing*) The cat's bowl.

*Enter June, Dorothy's younger sister, in a clerical collar and whatever archdeacons wear.*

(*Disappointed.*) Oh.

**June** Oh what?

**Dorothy** Is this mufti?

**June** Say again?

**Dorothy** Civvies. Now you're Archdeacon of Huddersfield I was looking forward to a touch of mauve.

**June** These days we keep the formality to a minimum.

**Dorothy** No cross even?

**June** Archdeacons are the accountants of the church. A cross is not always appropriate.

**Dorothy** Are you alone? Where's Mr Thing? The Trust man?

**June** I told Mr Lumsden to go round downstairs on his own. He'll come and see us when he's finished. He knows it's only a formality.

**Dorothy** How is Guthrie? Still breasting the billows?

**June** Very much so. She swam the Channel last week.

**Dorothy** Do you hear that, Iris? June's friend swam the Channel last week.

**Iris** What for? What happened to the boat?

**June** The homeless. Train now, anyway.

**Dorothy** It used to be such a performance swimming the Channel. Now it's like Everest. People do it after lunch.

**Iris** Big girl, is she?

**June** Not particularly.

**Iris** Is she a parson?

**June** She's a youth worker. Movement, gesture.

**Dorothy** Ah. Gesture.

**June** Who was that chap? We passed a car in the park.

**Dorothy** Nobody. Pest control.

**June** Yes. I saw a rat as I came in.

**Iris** Probably a mouse close to.

**June** The Trust will see to all that.

**Iris** He said that with the Trust we should be overrun.

**June** With rats?

**Iris** With people.

**June** What business is it of his?

**Dorothy** He was giving us tips on how to keep them out. Pest control.

**June** We've had this argument.

**Iris** Your sister is sitting on a gold mine apparently.
There's a fortune in the attics alone.

**Dorothy** Iris.

**Iris** Sorry.

**June** The attics? The attics? What was he doing up there?

**Iris** Telling us what we've got.

**June** We know what we've got.
  Was he a valuer – Sotheby's? Christie's?

**Dorothy** He was quite fetching. I was wishing Henry was
alive. Smelled wonderful.

**June** Of course he smelled wonderful. They do smell
wonderful. They're delicious in every respect but do you
know what they are – Sotheby's, Christie's, Bonham's?
Barrow boys.
  I thought we'd gone through all this. I just came over
today to dot the 'i's and cross the 't's to find you're still
flirting with Bond Street.

**Dorothy** Yes, and in the course of this so-called flirting it
emerges that you don't just give the house to the Trust.
I have to pay them to take it. It's called an . . .

**June** Endowment. I went through all that with you.
Provided the park comes with the house the endowment
can be waived.

**Dorothy** That's generous of them.

**June** It is. It *is*.

**Dorothy** I'd have been better off with the Japanese
golfers.

**June** Yes. Or the police college. Or the cookery school.
None of whom stumped up.

**Dorothy** It was the roof.

**June** It was the roof. It was the plumbing. It was the dry rot. It was the wet rot. It was the revelation that anyone fool enough to buy this place would have to take on the fabric and maintain it. It was the realisation that this perfect specimen of the genius of Robert Adam is on the verge of collapse. Nothing has been done to it for years. Henry did nothing. You've done nothing. It's just . . . static.

**Dorothy** Decay is a kind of progress.

**June** Dotty!

**Dorothy** I don't care. I would like to die here where I was born. Is that wrong?

**June** No, but it's a luxury. How many more times: death duties? And say you go first, who gets to pay them then? Me. I'm the Archdeacon of Huddersfield. I don't want to be married to this house.

**Iris** You won't get married to anything else. How is Guthrie? She must be a big girl to climb Everest.

**June** What are you knitting?

**Iris** Comforts for the troops.

**June** What troops?

**Iris** There are always troops.

**June** What you don't seem to understand is that if we don't give it to the Trust we'll be compelled to renovate the place ourselves and we do not have the money.

**Dorothy** So sell the Chippendale.

**June** *No.*
  It was made for the house.
  You never used to like the house.

**Dorothy** I don't like it or dislike it. It's home. Plus, there are no people. I spent half my life posing and being looked at. Well, not any more.

**June** There are no people now.

**Dorothy** Give it to the National Trust and there would be: in droves.

**June** People are unavoidable.

**Dorothy** I thought the clergy were supposed to like people.

**June** No, we're supposed to love them. Not the same.

**Dorothy** But you believe in God?

**June** This is the Church of England, that's not an issue.

**Dorothy** So do you still say your prayers?

**June** You used to say yours with that terrible rosary. Where is that? Where's that got to?

**Dorothy** I don't know, in a drawer somewhere.

**June** Because the Trust will want to know. That would be a star attraction, particularly these days?

**Dorothy** It won't be lost. It's got a luggage label on it.

**June** Where's Charles I's shirt?

*Dorothy shrugs.*

Don't you care?

**Dorothy** Yes, but they've survived because nobody did care. If they'd cared they'd have been sold years ago. I take them for granted. Not caring is what's preserved them.

**June** Henry took stuff for granted but his lorry drivers didn't; we lost stuff by the truck load, literally.

**Dorothy** Only at the finish.

**June** But wouldn't you like to see the place made presentable? The Adam rooms restored, the rubbish cleared out?

**Dorothy** Not if it means people traipsing round. There was a letter in the paper yesterday saying that the writer had been to York Minster and it was like King's Cross in the rush hour. None of them praying, needless to say. Just looking. And not even looking. Snapping it. Ticking it off. I don't want to be ticked off. And this was in 1983.

**June** Is that where you're up to? With the papers?

**Dorothy** There's a war on, near South America somewhere.

**Iris** Those troops. That's why I'm knitting.

**June** We won that war.

**Dorothy** You spoilsport. That takes all the fun out of it.

**June** It wasn't fun. Besides, there is – and I don't expect you to appreciate this – there is a moral case. We . . . our family . . .

**Dorothy** Oh, don't.

**June** We've been here since 1456.

**Iris** 1465.

**June** Isn't it time we made amends?

**Dorothy** What for?

**June** For the wool that built the house, the tenants turned off their land for sheep. After sheep it was iron and after iron, sugar, and sugar meant slaves. And after slaves, coal. Walk over the hill to where the colliery was and there's the business park. Somewhere . . . resited probably . . . there's a plaque to the ninety-three miners killed in an explosion just before the First War.

**Dorothy** That wasn't our fault. What has that got to do with us?

**June** Ours the colliery, ours the coal. Shawled wives gathered at the colliery gates; the empty cage coming up. All the ancient rituals of loss. Do we not owe for that?

*Ralph Lumsden has come in and overhears much of this speech.*

**Lumsden** Forgive me. I eavesdrop. But fascinating stuff. So rich. And the layered landscape. It is England. The history, the tragedy. And today, though one must not say so, the banality. A business park!

No, please, Lady Stacpoole, do not get up. I am after all a suitor, a suppliant. I crawl. Besides I want to envision you enthroned among your treasures. A picture of England. A *tableau vivant*. Ralph Lumsden.

**Dorothy** Yes. This is Iris, my . . .

**Iris** Companion.

**Lumsden** Oh, lady, lady, lady. One has been trying to see this house for so long. It throbs with history.

**Dorothy** Yes, though I think you may be under a misapprehension . . .

**June** My sister has a few minor reservations, but why don't you finish your tour of the house and then we can talk them through.

**Lumsden** Quite so. I'll just scoot round upstairs, though having seen the Adam rooms, no doubts, no doubts at all.

**June** Have you got a torch?

**Lumsden** I have. I am all 'tooled up'.

**Iris** Watch the floorboards.

**Lumsden** Have no fear. *À bientôt.*

*He goes off.*

**Dorothy** 'Minor reservations'.

**June** You changed your mind.

**Dorothy** I haven't changed it. Just not made it up yet.

**Iris** Tell her what the young feller said.

**June** Who?

**Iris** The man in the camel-hair coat.

**June** What about him? Dotty. What about him?

**Dorothy** Oh, Iris. (*She has let the cat out of the bag yet again.*) Nothing. Or nothing to do with the attic sale, anyway. It's some sort of group, people he knows who would restore the house, put me in the lodge and then move the whole place, lodge and all, to Wiltshire.

**June** Wiltshire?

**Dorothy** Dorset. Somewhere warm. They seem able to do what they like.

**June** I'd better meet this young man. He sounds a crook. Wiltshire? I don't know why I even care. I was never happy here, particularly after we had to get rid of the farm. Though Ralph says when the Trust gets the house they may bring back the farm and grow stuff for the café.

**Dorothy** Café? What café?

**June** There's always a café. The farm was why I ended up in the Church.

**Dorothy** The farm?

**June** When we were mucking out Henry would ponce down, wanting, as he put it, to help out, but actually to take a look at the new farmhand. Henry was useless. Easier to take the shovel and do it myself. Faffing about, that's what I can't stand. Men are useless . . . Henry with the shovel, the Archbishop of Canterbury with the synod.

**Iris** Do you still like a drink?

**June** Dear God. I was twelve years old.

**Iris** You couldn't stand up.

**June** Do we still have all that? The cellars?

**Dorothy** Henry did for most of it. Why?

**June** We could get Ralph a drink.

**Dorothy** I just want to do the right thing.

**June** It's too late. Doing the right thing isn't always the right thing to do. We have to get rid of the place.

**Dorothy** I'll go find a bottle.

**June** I can go. Is the key in the same place?

**Iris** You should know.

**Dorothy** Iris, behave. Some of it's under water.

*She goes. Pause.*

**June** So. How is Iris?

**Iris** Iris is all right.

**June** What do you feel about the house?

**Iris** She'll do what she wants to do. You'll do what you want to do. No change there. Fratch. Fratch. Fratch.

**June** Does she talk ever?

*Iris says nothing.*

It was the baby that started it.

**Iris** It wasn't a baby. It hadn't got that far.
All that stuff about us owing for this house, being the wicked landowners, the mine and whatnot . . . you don't honestly believe all that? It's just what people say.

**June**  You wouldn't understand.

**Iris**  Oh, I think I do.

Your love affair with the National Trust, when did that start?

**June**  I've always been in favour.

**Iris**  No, you haven't. Not when you were young. When you tippled to the fact that if Henry died it was Dotty who would inherit the place and not you, you were mad as anything.

When she had scarlet fever and was really poorly you were in and out of that room, taking her temperature every five minutes.

**June**  I was a child. I wanted to be a nurse.

**Iris**  You wanted her out of the way; if Henry died this would all go to her.

Henry does die; enter the National Trust.

**June**  Correction. Henry dies. The estate pays a fortune in death duties. That was when the Trust came into the picture.

**Iris**  You say.

**June**  I know.

**Iris**  You can't have it, so it has to go to the nation: everybody has to have it. Does he know about the coal?

**June**  All in good time.

*Dorothy, now in gumboots, comes back, shaking her head.*

**Dorothy**  Found the key at least. Can't open the door.

**June**  I'll go.

*She goes.*

**Dorothy** (*holding up a string of brown beads with a luggage label attached*) Look.

*They examine them together.*

**Iris** They do look just like beads. Where were they?

**Dorothy** In the same drawer as the cellar key. In a bit of newspaper. Where I must have put them, I suppose. Dreadful. Clicked through those swollen fingers.

*She shudders but puts them on, hiding them under her dress.*

Don't say anything to her. And don't say anything to him.

*She sneaks another look.*

Amber, I suppose. And the coat of arms, look.

*Lumsden returns.*

**Lumsden** My torch seems to have given up the ghost. And I can't open the shutters. Still, I've seen all that I need. Besides, I have to return to the present. Because it casts a spell. Not on you . . . you are part of the spell . . . but on those fortunate enough to be given a glimpse of . . . all this.

**Dorothy** How kind.

**Lumsden** Forgive me if I enthuse, but I see this house and your family's continuous occupancy of it as a metaphor. Tell a child the story of England and it is all here.

**Dorothy** Yes. I would be deceiving you, Mr Lumsden, if I said I had not heard such twaddle before.
  I particularly abhor metaphor.
  Metaphor is fraud.
  England with all its faults.
  A country house with all its shortcomings.
  The one is not the other . . . however much the Trust

would like us to think so. I will not collaborate in your conceit of country. It is a pretend England.

**Lumsden** Oh. This is a surprise. I must marshal my forces. I suppose I would say that we . . . the Trust, its houses, its coastline, its landscape . . . are, if not the model of England, at least its mitigation.

**Dorothy** Country houses are window dressing. They mitigate nothing.

**Lumsden** Does this affect your donation?

**June** (*returning with the bottle*) No, of course it doesn't. My sister sits alone in this mouldering house and gets some cockeyed ideas.

**Lumsden** Now, Lady Dorothy, we like to debrief our donors. I want you to tell me everything.

**Dorothy** Nothing to tell. This is not the Cotswolds, Mr Lumsden, and South Yorkshire is not conducive to anecdote. We lived as we live now, in a fraction of the house. We did not hunt. The miners had a livelier time than we did, our one excitement when the Festival Ballet came to Sheffield.

**Iris** And the open-cast mining. That came right up to the terrace.

**Dorothy** But no legends. No idylls. Nothing you could market. And no one the least larger than life.

**Lumsden** There is one legend. I've always understood that what is reputed to be here is the rosary belonging to Henry VIII.

**June** It's here somewhere.

**Dorothy** Yes. I saw it when I was a child and indeed used to play with it. Now . . .

*She shakes her head.*

**June** It must be here.

**Iris** Everything is here somewhere.

**Lumsden** I'm sure, and of course the first thing we would want to do is make an inventory about what we've . . . what you've got.

But not aspic. Not aspic at all. Back in the day, yes, red ropes. 'Do not touch'. Everything in its place. Nowadays the scullery and the still room are as important as the drawing room. And we interact . . . racks of costumes, frock coats, doublets . . . Visitors can feel themselves a part of the house.

But no pretence. I noticed for instance as I went round the ragged footings of the tapestries . . . gnawed by mice, and wet by centuries of dogs. What we would hope to do is to have our experts clean them, obviously with a degree of stabilisation but making no attempt at repair. Or even disguise. Rather we would draw visitors' attention to them, focus on them as part of the history of the house. They are after all a testament to time and its abrasions. And we cannot halt time . . . but we can put it on hold – while we live in the present.

I won't, thank you.

*June is offering him a drink.*

**June** I don't want to drink on my own.

**Iris** It's never stopped you before.

**Dorothy** Iris.
Mr Lumsden. I have lived in this house all my life.

**June** Well, that's not true for a start. There was a long period when you never came near. You were gallivanting about in London and Paris and New York. So not quite all your life.

**Lumsden** Archdeacon.

**Dorothy** I came back here when I was in trouble. It is where I want to die.

**Lumsden** If the Trust accepts the property of course you can stay here. You must stay here. Your own little flat furnished with your own favourite pieces plus a chintz of your choice.

**Dorothy** You say, 'If the Trust accepts the property.' My sister implied you had no doubts.

**Lumsden** I don't. How could I? A soldier returns from the Hundred Years War and builds a house. On the lawns of the same house five centuries later the survivors of Dunkirk are nursed back to health. It's a story and a story the house longs to tell . . . I can almost smell it.

**Iris** She won't open the windows.

**Lumsden** However, we are a large organisation. Top of my wish list though this is, it's only fair to tell you there is a school of thought on my committee that thinks we have enough country houses as it is. Do we need another? Yes, I say. This is special. And it's been so ever since I came across the only photographs of it I've ever seen in an old *Country Life* when I was a boy.

**Dorothy** It won't look like that now.

**Lumsden** Well, it does rather. But money is tight and there are other contenders in the field. The childhood home of Cilla Black and . . . the past lapping always at the feet of the present . . . a pithead baths in Featherstone plus the last functioning children's library in the north-east.

And unlike them what weighs against this house is that it isn't in any sense 'of the people'. And of course it's a big ask.

**Dorothy** A 'big ask' what?

**June** A tall order.

**Lumsden** It will be expensive to restore. Another acquisition under discussion are some surviving cells from the Maze prison in Belfast . . . cells which figured in the so-called dirty protest. Do we, how shall I put it, save them? Do we restore the patina? I think we do. I think we must. But you see our dilemma.

**Dorothy** (*cheerfully*) Oh, so you're not sure you want it after all?

**Lumsden** Oh no, dear lady. We do, we do. We must.

**Dorothy** Because one has had interest elsewhere. Someone came to look at the attics only this morning.

**Lumsden** I don't like the sound of that.

**June** It was nothing. Bicycles, croquet mallets . . . it was only the junk.

**Lumsden** Archdeacon, I beg to differ. Bicycles and croquet mallets are not junk. I would go so far as to say they are the very essence of it. Bicycles and croquet mallets are what the Trust is about. A Sheraton side table or an Edwardian mangle . . . no comparison. But which gives a livelier sense of the heart of the house and the life lived here? No. I beg you. We must keep the place intact. It's a wonderful house and I long to see it brought back to life. There are some intriguing oddities . . . the attic rooms full of old newspapers, for instance.

**June** Oh, you could clear those out tomorrow.

**Dorothy** NO!

**Lumsden** Another oddity, in the Adam saloon . . .

**June** I think I know what's coming. I should have told you about this. I can explain.

**Lumsden** Please. You sound as if you expect me to be shocked. I wasn't shocked at all. I felt I was perhaps being more nosy at this stage than perhaps I'm entitled to be – this was only a preliminary perambulation after all – but behind the Gothick tracery in the Adam saloon one happened upon a cupboard . . .

**Dorothy** Not a cupboard. A closet.

**June** Oh God.

**Lumsden** There are . . . I may have misunderstood . . . but rows and rows . . . I should have said about two dozen in all . . . of chamber pots. Full chamber pots . . .

**Dorothy** Did you take any of them down?

**Lumsden** I didn't feel it was my place.

**Dorothy** So you didn't look underneath?

**Lumsden** Hardly. They were quite full. And a touch . . . unsavoury.

**Iris** Well, you daft thing, you should have looked underneath.

**Lumsden** Why? What's inside?

**June** Well . . . urine, of course. Ancient urine.

**Dorothy** And having with due care and attention looked underneath you'd have found labels. With names.

**Lumsden** Names?

**Dorothy** Rudyard Kipling, Ramsay MacDonald, George Bernard Shaw, Thomas Hardy . . .

**Iris** T. E. Lawrence.

**Lumsden** Fascinating. To what purpose?

**Iris** Lord Halifax.

**Dorothy** It's always been known as the Adam saloon since the time when Adam designed it. Only in the nineteenth century and after it was used as a billiard room . . . and would be still, only we had to take the billiard table upstairs to the attic on account of the roof . . . there's a tin bath on it at the moment.

**Lumsden** I saw.

**Iris** Osbert Sitwell.

**Dorothy** The saloon is a long way from the downstairs lav so when they were playing billiards after dinner they would use individual chamber pots. And if they were at all celebrated . . . Shaw, Hardy, Mr Asquith . . . they weren't emptied.

**June** Absurd. It's worse than absurd: it's embarrassing.

**Iris** Lord Linlithgow.

**Lumsden** Really? Well . . . who was he?

**Iris** I don't know, but his name's on a po so he must have been somebody.

**Dorothy** The one absentee is Henry James, who often stayed here, but he was too fastidious to use the chamber pot, insisted on making the long trek to the loo.

**Lumsden** Oh dear. What a shame!

**Iris** Yes, and it held the game up.

**June** While we're talking about the saloon I might bring somebody diocesan round to see it, as is.

**Dorothy** Who?

**June** The Bishop.

**Dorothy** What is the Bishop?

*June looks askance.*

A he or a she?

**June** Regrettably at this moment in time the episcopacy is wholly male. But there is movement. It's only a matter of time before women seize the crozier and the gaiter yields to the garter.

**Dorothy** Oh, treats!

**June** And I have to say, fond of the Gothick though he is, Mervyn, our bishop, is not unfrisky and the vestry has seen several awkward moments. That was before Guthrie came along, of course.

**Iris** Of course.

**Lumsden** Has anyone ever written about the saloon or done it for TV?

**Dorothy** Certainly not. We don't have any of that. No TV. There's a wireless somewhere just in case.

**Lumsden** Just in case what?

**Dorothy** War. The last one they had to send down to the kitchen to listen to Mr Chamberlain.

**Iris** He came here once.

**Lumsden** Any wee?

**Iris** Didn't play billiards.

**Lumsden** That is fascinating. I am captivated. I was certain as I went round that this house was for us, but I didn't know why. Architecturally it's extraordinary – the pictures, the furniture – but it needed one more feature to make it special.

**June** The chamber pots?

**Lumsden** And the newspapers . . . They were the clues, and I now begin to see how I can make the case for the house to my people. Thank you. Thank you.

**June** Jolly good. I don't altogether understand why, but the house has obviously ticked the right boxes.

**Lumsden** Some unique boxes. And I'll be in touch very shortly.

**Dorothy** One moment. Flattered though I am that with all its shortcomings you like the house . . . I have to tell you . . .

**June** Dotty . . .

**Dorothy** No. I *will* speak. My sister has misled you.

**June** We can talk this over. Not now.

**Dorothy** While I would happily hand over the house to be kept up as it is, what I do not want is for the place to be overrun with droves of visitors.

**Lumsden** People are ineluctable, Lady Dorothy. They are endemic. They are unavoidable.
  While of course as a growth organisation we are concerned to maximise our percentage footfall, do please bear in mind these are not just people. Our membership is made up of self-selecting individuals who appreciate the art and craftsmanship of the past.

**Dorothy** And who just want somewhere to go.

**Lumsden** But nothing will change.

**Dorothy** The *looking* will change it. Looking always does.

**June** How many more times, Dotty, there is no other way. We would like you to have the house.

**Iris** You would. She wouldn't. No 'we' about it.

**June** It's the only way.

**Dorothy** It's not the only way. I have other irons in the fire.

**June** Dorothy.

**Dorothy** I had a better offer only this morning.

**Lumsden** A better offer? Are we in competition?

**June** No. *No.*

**Dorothy** I'm currently waiting for them to get back to me.

**Lumsden** I knew I had to persuade my people, but you assured me your sister had made up her mind.

**June** She had. She has.

**Iris** You were always a madam; she hasn't.

**Lumsden** This is dreadful. I need a decision. I can't go back to the committee with a maybe. It's heartbreaking. This . . . it's England. You are its custodian. We mustn't lose it.

**Dorothy** No. I'm not England. I just live here. Goodbye, Mr Lumsden.

**Lumsden** I despair. Sad, sad, sad. (*To June.*) I will telephone.

**June** I'll come out with you.

> *They are going out, but June lets him get ahead before turning back and saying deliberately:*

You – stupid – cow.

> *She is going off again when she has another thought, comes back and takes the opened bottle before finally going.*

And don't forget. I've got the Bishop coming.

> *Dorothy remains in her chair, catching the occasional moth before dozing off. Iris, seeing she is asleep, gathers up her things and goes.*

**Dorothy** Bloody man.

England is not my problem. I will not be metaphorised.
This is not Allegory House.
England not.
History not.
Bring it on.

*She dozes.*

*Time passes.*

*There is the sound of a distant window breaking, but
Dorothy doesn't wake. (Or does she wake and fall over?)*

*After a while a large suave figure appears. He is
elegantly dressed and is entirely at ease, slightly
younger than Dorothy.*

*Mr Theodore, coat over shoulders, arms not in
sleeves, wanders round. Then he spots Dorothy lying
on the floor.*

**Theodore** Dear me. Are you all right? Have you been
here long?

**Dorothy** Since 1456. How did you get in?

**Theodore** I don't know. It was some sort of pantry. Are
you alone here?

**Dorothy** Yes. Well, I'm saying alone . . . People are
popping in all the time. The place is teeming. And I'm not
alone at night either.

**Theodore** A lady of such charm . . . I should hope not.

**Dorothy** I didn't mean that.

**Theodore** What did you mean? (*He is looking around.*)

**Dorothy** I mean people sleep here, big people, strong.
People you wouldn't want to get on the wrong side of,
those kind of people.

**Theodore** Oh yes. They're the best. I like those kind of
people myself.

**Dorothy** I was told to expect someone.

**Theodore** One should always expect someone, don't you think? It keeps one . . . on one's toes.

**Dorothy** That's right. One forgets.
So are you the person?

**Theodore** I could be.

**Dorothy** You're not a burglar?

*He laughs. She laughs.*

One has to ask. Insurance and so on.

**Theodore** No. I'm not a burglar. In fact, I have a card somewhere. (*He vaguely looks.*) But you're by yourself here . . . apart from the –

**Dorothy** – big men, yes. Might one know your name?

**Theodore** Theodore.

**Dorothy** And is that your first name or your last?

**Theodore** Both if necessary.

**Dorothy** Come into the light.

*Pause.*

Is this a coincidence?

**Theodore** I'm sorry?

**Dorothy** Did you know where I was?
Look at me.
Ring any bells?
'*Non e vero, Contessa*'?

**Theodore** Lofty! Oh my goodness!
I had no idea.
It was just a house.

**Dorothy** Oh. So you are a burglar?

**Theodore** No.

*He finds his card and gives it to her.*

**Dorothy** What's this 'Mr Theodore'? What happened to Teddy?

**Theodore** It's what I'm called now.

**Dorothy** 'Locations Manager. Films. Commercials.'
(*She looks at him.*) And *smart*!
Me, I'm a bit of a sight.

**Theodore** I've seen you better.
Who were you waiting for? You thought I was someone else.

**Dorothy** Nobody important. Teddy.
What sort of films?

**Theodore** We're a small specialised outfit. We had a location over at Easingwold but it fell through.

**Dorothy** You had lovely legs.

**Theodore** We both did.
This would be ideal, only we're on a shoestring. We could only offer you £5,000 or so.

**Dorothy** Oh. Peanuts.

**Theodore** In cash of course. It would take a week. Ten days at the most.
Why are you smiling?

**Dorothy** You were a boy. Now you're . . .

**Theodore** Don't say it. A tea boy. I didn't think you'd even noticed me.

**Dorothy** Oh yes. And your legs.

**Theodore** Nobody ever knew, did they? You were so grand. I was nobody.

**Dorothy** And you were so young, so we never went anywhere.

**Theodore** Or if we did it was with Clive from make-up. People thought I was his boyfriend, not yours.

*Iris comes in.*

**Theodore** Is this the heavy mob?

**Dorothy** This is Iris, my . . .

**Iris** Companion.

**Theodore** So when do the big boys arrive?

**Dorothy** Who?

**Theodore** The ones who take care of you during the hours of darkness.

**Dorothy** Oh, you never see them. That's the mark of a good servant . . . they keep out of the way. The Queen thinks she's alone in Buckingham Palace.

*Theodore laughs. She laughs. They are flirting.*

This gentleman is making a film.

**Iris** Yes. He looks the type.

**Dorothy** Do you want to see the house?

**Theodore** Not particularly. It seems perfect.

**Dorothy** It is. The National Trust have had their eye on it. And other people. Have you ever filmed in one of their houses?

**Theodore** No. they're a bit too . . . uptight.

**Dorothy** Respectable?

**Theodore** Quite. You're not respectable then?

**Dorothy** You've forgotten, I'm a peeress in my own right. The middle class, they're the respectable ones.

**Theodore** What happened to your baby?

**Iris** It wasn't a baby.

**Dorothy** It was to me.

**Iris** It hadn't got that far.

**Theodore** I'm sorry.

**Iris** Don't be silly. It was forty years ago.

**Dorothy** Forty-six.

**Theodore** Who was the father?

**Dorothy** Not you, alas.
  Some photographer.

**Theodore** What was his name?

**Dorothy** Parker.

**Theodore** Oh him. You dirty girl.

  *He consults his iPod.*

**Dorothy** Oh. You've got one of those things. Does everybody?

**Theodore** Pretty much.
  Dead apparently, Parker.

**Dorothy** No? Oh dear.

**Theodore** You didn't like him?

**Dorothy** He was a joke. What a man asks of a woman is that she take him seriously. I never could.

**Theodore** You did me.

**Dorothy** It was the legs.

I didn't want to be a model any more. The baby was going to be my 'Get Out of Jail Free' card. When it didn't happen I went off my rocker for a bit. And then just sat here.

**Theodore** Lofty.

**Dorothy** I thought something would happen. Marriage or something, only it never did. It took me ages . . . years to realise it was for me to make it happen. Too late.

**Theodore** No.

**Dorothy** You . . . you made it happen . . . you're a film producer.

**Theodore** Remember this.

*Dorothy puts his iPod to her ear and starts to sing along. Music from the fifties – 'The Blacksmith Blues' or 'Do Not Forsake Me, O My Darling' – even 'This Nearly Was Mine' from* South Pacific.
*They dance.*

**Dorothy** So. Will there be actors?

**Theodore** Of a sort.

**Dorothy** That's fun. The arrival of the players.

**Theodore** There's just one more thing. Do you have a four-poster bed?

**Dorothy** Oh *yes*. Several.

**Theodore** Brilliant. Let's have a look. Come along, Stacpoole.

*She laughs. She knows everything.*

# Act Two

*The stage is dark, the outlines of the room just visible with some chinks of light round the windows. Two figures cautiously make their way across the room.*

**Bishop** Archdeacon?

**June** Bishop?

**Bishop** It's dark. Could I hold your hand?

**June** Is that wise?

**Bishop** No, no. You don't understand, I'm struggling with some new bifocals.

**June** Of course you are.

**Bishop** Where is it?

**June** What?

**Bishop** Your hand.

**June** Here, here.

**Bishop** Ah, thank you. What happened to the lights, do you think? Why are the shutters closed?

**June** It's on account of the tapestries.

*She guides him.*

A step up. Here we are. The Adam rooms are through here.

**Bishop** The promised land.

*She opens a door, they go through and she closes the door. There is a moment of silence and darkness, then the room is flooded with much stronger light and the*

*windows are revealed as shrouded in blackout material
and lighting set up all ready for filming as the crew
come in from breakfast/lunch. Theodore and Bruce,
the grip, on stage.*

**Bruce** Fuck me. You have to admit, boss – it is Catpiss
Hall.

**Theodore** Oh, I don't know. This bit's quite cosy. Better
than where we were in the Long Gallery.

**Bruce** It's just as filthy.

**Theodore** It's meant to be filthy. Filthy is favourite.

**Bruce** Yeah, but you know me. I like to start off clean.
If it has to be filthified I prefer to apply it myself out of
a can. Besides. real muck just looks tacky. A whole
philosophy there. boss: what's real looks false, the
genuine is what you counterfeit . . .

**Theodore** Well, let's hope we can counterfeit some
genuine sex.

*A call of 'Bed coming through!' as bits of a four-poster
bed come through.*

Now, Bruce. You're a nancy, what period is all this?

*Bruce considers.*

Georgian?

**Bruce** This? Naw. More Inigo Jones, though it might be
Peter Jones for all you know. Lovely in there. Adam. An
early essay in the Gothick.

**Theodore** But what do you think?

**Bruce** It's shit-heapness apart, you mean? I'd give it a
seven.

*Iris comes in and sits down.*

You can't sit there, darling.

**Iris** I always sit here. This is my seat.

*Bruce lifts Iris, seat and all, and moves her out of the way of the incoming bed.*

I liked that. Could we do it again? It's a long time since I've seen someone like you.

**Theodore** What?

**Iris** Big. Mind you, we've had them in the past.

**Theodore** I'm glad to hear it.

**Iris** In the war. When the Canadians came. Some of them were on the big side.

**Theodore** Yes?

**Iris** But they were very polite. Big and polite, that's what you want.

*Dorothy comes downstairs, swathed in a fluffy white dressing gown, head in a towel, white pompom slippers.*

**Dorothy** Iris, you're to come upstairs and have a bath this minute.

**Iris** What would I be doing with a bath?

**Dorothy** I've just had one and it's heaven, so no more nonsense.

**Iris** Where did you get that dressing gown?

**Dorothy** It's a prop apparently, the slippers too.

**Iris** Wasn't it cold?

**Dorothy** No, silly. Suddenly the plumbing works. After forty years. Can't you feel it? Oh Mr Theodore, you are It.

*Theodore modestly indicates Bruce.*

And thank you, Mr Grip. The radiators upstairs are boiling. What did you do?

**Bruce** Well, I lit the boiler for a start.

**Dorothy** Is that what you're supposed to do?

**Bruce** It helps.

**Iris** Don't get piles.

**Dorothy** Mr Grip says the boiler was cattled but now it's practical apparently, though what they're using for fuel I can't think.

Did you have your breakfast?

**Iris** They fetched it me. In the Painted Room of all places. I said there is a proper breakfast room, only it's full of Henry's bottles so they said the Painted Room made more sense. I sat on the bed. I said Oliver Cromwell slept in this bed. They said not with you? The food is nice only they're cheeky.

**Louise** (*from off*) Iris!

**Dorothy** (*calling upstairs*) She's coming. Mr Theodore, can I stay and watch?

**Theodore** In any other circumstances I would be delighted but it's what we call a closed set.

**Dorothy** If you say so. I'm having such a heavenly time. I wouldn't want to spoil it.

**Iris** I had porridge, bacon, haddock and fried potatoes.

**Dorothy** I had the vegetarian option. Cauliflower cheese.

**Iris** I had that too. It can't last. I've put some of the fried potatoes in my bag just in case.

**Louise** (*entering*) Dorothy, we need to do your hair. Iris, you're to have your bath so we can put on your costume.

**Iris** What costume? I don't have a costume.

**Louise** You do now.

**Dorothy** We must do as we're told. Is it period?

44

**Louise** Well, it's periodesque.

*They go upstairs. Dorothy runs her hand along some
surface.*

So clean! Adorable. Lovely Mr Grip.

**Theodore** All clear. Look sharp.

**Nigel** Come on. Chop chop, you two.

*The actors come in plus a skeleton crew.
Brit (twenty-five), a Latvian girl, and Colin (thirties),
English, both in dressing gowns.*

**Colin** All I am saying is you can't get a hard-on with
hypothermia. Hypothermia and a hard-on don't go hand
in hand.

**Theodore** You're supposed to be a professional.

**Colin** I used to be an actor.

**Theodore** Anyway, it's warming up.

**Colin** I wish I was.

**Nigel** (*the assistant director*) Keep it together. Brit, are
you ready?

**Brit** (*who has been positioned on the bed*) Brit ready. Brit
ready long time.

**Nigel** Colin?

*Colin is looking at a magazine and is also on his mobile.*

**Colin** Getting there.

**Theodore** How're you doing?

**Colin** (*texting*) Not sure.

**Theodore** Well, why don't you get on the mobile to your
dick and find out.

**Nigel** (*in an undertone*) Did you not take a pill?

**Colin** I took one yesterday. I don't like to take one every time. I'm a vegan.

**Nigel** (*under his breath*) Oh for fuck's sake. Final checks.

**Colin** Nigel. Can she not knit?

**Nigel** Brit, love. Can you not knit?

**Brit** I can knit, yes. I knit, see. Brit love to knit.

**Nigel** No, not. Not knit.

**Brit** Latvia is cold country. Riga is cold climate. Brit knit tights for grandmother.

**Colin** But not *now*.

**Nigel** OK. Gowns off.

**Brit** Brit no knit.

**Colin** Thank you.

**Nigel** Bruce, are you happy?

**Brit** Colin. I hope you wash private parts.

**Colin** Oh God.

**Les** (*the cameraman*) Nigel. Can you put a slate on?

*He does so.*
*The action (i.e. the sex) should be upstage and largely obscured by the camera and crew standing round.*

**Brit** Can Brit have direction please?

**Theodore** Yes?

**Brit** Brit is virgin? It is first time? It is first time Brit does it?

**Theodore** Yes. And this is supposed to be the first one you've seen.

*Brit gestures towards Colin's dick.*

46

**Brit** È. Poor Brit.

**Theodore** And Colin, sweetheart. A gnat's more interested. Displayed before you and wholly at your disposal is that fragrant chasm to which men have tended since the dawn of time. Here it is . . . the golden gate, the portals of ecstasy and you are looking at it as if it's a plate of cold rice pudding.

**Brit** Is rice pudding?

**Theodore** No.

**Brit** He eat rice pudding off Brit's private parts? I was Sunday School teacher.

**Theodore** Brit. There is no rice pudding.
There is sexual intercourse.
There is dick.
There is no rice pudding.

*Pause.*

**Brit** (*hopefully*) Is treacle pudding?

**Theodore** For fuck's sake can you just copulate. Turn over.

**Les** Speed. Mark it.

**Nigel** Silence.

**Bruce** Sound rolling.

**Nigel** *Reach for the Thigh.* Slate 35, Take 1.

**Theodore** Action.

*Pause, while some seemingly ineffectual sex happens, watched by Theodore on the monitor.*

Cut. Les. Can you try another angle?

**Les** The angle of the camera is not the problem –

**Brit** Is no good. Is coming in and is going out, but is all flip-flop.

**Bruce** It's like trying to get a Pontefract cake into a slot machine.

**Theodore** What did it look like?

**Les** It looks like marriage. Mine anyway.

**Theodore** Oh God. All I'm asking for is an appearance of concupiscence. Give Colin something to read, somebody.

**Colin** (*with magazines*) Seen that, seen that. If we invested in some fresh reading matter it might help.

*Brit has put on her dressing gown, as has Colin.*

**Nigel** (*handing him a pill*) Here, have one of mine.

**Colin** No, I've told you.

**Nigel** No problem. This is organic.

*Colin takes it.*

**Les** (*to Theodore*) I can't shoot what's not there.

**Theodore** Keep an eye open for madam. (*He is looking through the script.*)

**Nigel** I thought she knew.

**Theodore** Who knows what she knows?
Actually . . . we could do her scene while we're waiting for wood. Louise, are the girls ready?
Change of plan. Get Colin and Brit dressed.

**Louise** Give me a second.

**Theodore** Change of plan. Get Colin and Brit dressed.

**Nigel** Scene 16A.

**Theodore** Shooting from here.

*Louise runs upstairs. There is a pause.*

**Louise** (*off*) Wait for it . . .

**Theodore**  Oh my Lord.

*Dorothy enters (and it is a definite entrance). She enters resplendent in a fifties couture (or Fortuny) dress, made-up, hair done and looking wonderful and young. Maybe even with fifties music ('Knightsbridge March' or somesuch).*

*Applause. Someone takes a photograph. Iris brings up the rear, disgruntled and dressed as a ladies' maid.*

**Theodore**  Louise, it's a triumph.

**Dorothy**  It's not just Louise.

**Louise**  We didn't know which number to choose there are so many.

**Dorothy**  One has to be able to carry it off. The others used to simper. I was always very stern. Lofty, they used to call me.

**Theodore**  (*kisses her hand*) Dear Lofty.

**Dorothy**  Though remember I can't act.

Norman Parkinson said I could act as far as the end of the catwalk before I became a frightened rabbit. But isn't this fun? I can't remember when I last had fun.

**Louise**  Still not sure about those beads.

**Dorothy**  I am.

**Louise**  You've got heaps of nicer things. They aren't even in period.

**Theodore**  Never mind. With luck nobody's going to be thinking about beads.

*Bruce fingers the dress.*

**Bruce**  Dior?

**Dorothy**  What a divine man! Plumbing and haute couture. Though it's actually Balenciaga.

**Bruce** Damn.

**Dorothy** And the wrap?

**Bruce** Oh come on, don't insult me. Schiaparelli.

**Colin** (*an offstage shout*) Bruce!

**Bruce** But banishing all thoughts of Schiaparelli I must go unblock a sink.

**Theodore** So this is the scene. The girl is on the bed. Brit. Nigel, the maid.

**Nigel** This way, darling.

**Theodore** Dorothy brings in the young man, *comme ça.* Escorts him to the bed where she shows him the girl, then tactfully withdraws. Whereupon the young man takes off his trousers. Etcetera

**Dorothy** What am I?

**Theodore** You . . . well . . . you're an ex-woman of the world.

**Iris** And what am I . . . the companion?

**Dorothy** No. The maid.

**Iris** So no change there then.

**Dorothy** And do I speak?

**Theodore** Nobody speaks. We're not on sound.

**Les** Nigel, could you move Grandma up a bit? Could our Baltic friend move a tad to the left? Perfect.

**Theodore** Let's try a rehearsal. Off you go

*They go through the action. Very stilted.*

Dorothy, a gnat's less discretion . . . whereas Brit . . . try and look more demure.

**Brit** What is this demure?

**Dorothy** Bashful. (*And shows her.*)

**Theodore** And Dorothy withdraw.

**Nigel** Grandma –

**Theodore** Right. Going for one.

**Nigel** Back you come, Grandma.

**Les** Rolling.

**Theodore** Mark it

**Nigel** *Reach for the Thigh*. Slate 36, Take 1.

**Les** Speed.

**Theodore** Action.

> *They do it with Colin making a move on Brit as soon as Dorothy starts to withdraw.*

Cut. Perfect. How was it for you, Les?

> *Les gives a thumbs up.*

**Dorothy** Because I'm happy to do it again.

**Theodore** No. On we go. Back to Scene 36. Colin, any joy?

**Colin** Give me a minute.

> *He gets some new magazines and retires to the sofa.*

**Theodore** Les once worked with David Lean.

**Bruce** Did you, Les?

**Les** Yeah. For about five minutes.

**Bruce** What was he like?

**Les** He was a prick.

**Theodore** Still, it was film. And this is film. (*He pats the camera.*) Not some digital rubbish any wanky boy could run up in the back bedroom.

**Bruce** There, there, big man.

**Theodore** Yes. I'm just a sentimental arsehole.

**Les** Oh, I wouldn't have said you were sentimental.

**Theodore** We have to resist the threat of the internet. What I'm after, Les, is higher production values for the couples market. Filthy but tasteful.

**Dorothy** There's a lot of hanging about, isn't there? Mind you, I'm used to that. Fashion was the same. And war, too, so I'm told.

*She sits by Colin.*

You do like reading, don't you?

**Colin** Sometimes.

**Dorothy** I've seen you once or twice, having a bit of time to yourself. What is it you're reading?

**Colin** Oh, this and that.

*Louise takes her aside.*

**Louise** You shouldn't talk to Colin.

**Dorothy** Why? He seems a nice young man.

**Louise** He's working.

**Dorothy** No, he isn't. He's reading. I heard somebody say we were waiting for Wood. He seems very unpunctual. They were waiting for him yesterday. Where is he?

**Louise** He's on his way.

**Iris** Do they say they want some wood?

**Louise**  No.

**Iris**  Because there's loads in the stables. Once upon a time we had a boy just for that. He was killed at Arnhem.

**Louise**  Perhaps I can put you into something else.

**Dorothy**  Anything, darling. It's such fun! (*Smelling herself.*) And I'm so clean, Louise. Did I smell? Before?

**Louise**  A bit.

**Dorothy**  Iris too, I imagine.

**Louise**  Worse.

**Dorothy**  Lovely now. And this. I feel like I used to be.

**Louise**  Balenciaga again? Or Hardy Amies?

**Dorothy**  Hardy Amies. Heaven! Oh look, he's got his trousers off again! What treats!

*They go upstairs.*

**Nigel**  How's it going?

*Colin gives him the thumbs-up.*

**Colin**  What is it?

**Nigel**  Herbs. But then it's all herbs basically. (*He sniffs.*)

**Colin**  It works. The wonders of chemistry.

**Theodore**  Are we all set, Nigel? That looks quite presentable, Colin. She can't complain about that. Les?

**Nigel**  Slate 36, Take 1.

**Theodore**  Take it slowly and – action.

*He watches on the screen while giving directions.*

Tits. Lovely.

**Brit** This is very pleasant, no? Now we are gas cooking. I excite already. I am groaning.

**Theodore** Kiss her, Colin. *Kiss* her.
Tell the story, Les, tell the story.
Brilliant.
And the other way about.
Get rid of your leg, Colin, we're not interested in your knee.

*During this, Iris has appeared. She tries to see over the heads of the crew but doesn't manage it and then notices Theodore's monitor. He doesn't notice her at first as, tilting her head this way and that, she tries to figure out what's happening.*

**Iris** What're they doing?

**Theodore** She's passed out. He's resuscitating her.

**Iris** I've never heard it called that. It happened to me once, years ago. The same thing, I was resuscitated.
They used to do it a lot in the war.

**Theodore** I'm sure.

**Iris** They were resuscitating all over the park. But then they were Canadians.

**Les** And Grandma, less bunny.

*Theodore gestures to Nigel to get her out of the way.*

**Theodore** Now some heavy-duty stuff. Give it some welly. Yes. Yes. More of that. Good.

*Brit is groaning.*
*At which point June and the Bishop come into view, about to enter the scene, though nobody taking part notices, so they continue screwing and filming.*
*Dorothy in some stunning new outfit takes in the scene, screwing included, and the new arrivals, as June sees what is going on and is aghast.*

54

**Bishop** And you say it's going to the National Trust.

**June** We hope.

**Bishop** Pity. It would have made a splendid theological college.

Now. What is going on here?

**Dorothy** Bishop. Bishop. Welcome. Welcome. What a pleasure to see you.

**Bishop** Lady Stacpoole.

**June** (*first sight of Dorothy's frock*) What is all this? What is going on?

**Dorothy** I know! I'm afraid at present things are a little *mouvementé*.

**Bishop** Yes. I'm struggling with some new bifocals. I can't quite see.

*Dorothy puts her finger to her lips.*

**Dorothy** It's the Women's Institute.

**Bishop** An admirable body of women. And fearless. What are they doing?

**Dorothy** What are they doing? The Women's Institute? They're shooting their Advent Calendar.

**Bishop** Really? Oh I adore those calendars. Ample ladies of unimpeachable morals, their salient features artfully occluded. Never has the Marigold glove been better deployed.

**Bruce** I'm loving your frock.

**Bishop** Oh, how kind.

Am I right or are one or two hubbies here as well? Jolly good.

**June** Bishop.

**Bishop** Well, we must love you and leave you.

More power to your elbow.

(*As they are going.*) You said your sister was eccentric. She's a *charming* woman.

*June turns back.*

**June** (*murderously*) Animals!

**Theodore** (*after a livid look from the departing June*) Something tells me this is going to be Easingwold all over again.

**Nigel** What?

**Theodore** A w-r-a-p.

**Nigel** *and* **Others** Oh no. / Not again. (*Etc.*)

**Theodore** Still, I think we got it. Happy, Les?

**Les** Ecstatic.

**Theodore** Why, what was wrong with that?

**Les** I didn't get the reverse.

**Theodore** I think they'll get the picture. It's not *Citizen Kane.*

Right, boys and girls. This is what's known as a wrap.

*A lot of activity clearing up. While in the foreground Theodore and Dorothy talk.*

**Dorothy** How did you get into this?

**Theodore** Like anything else. I was a player. Then, when I ceased to be a player, I went into management. It started off as fun.

**Dorothy** Modelling the same. But that's the way of it. Sooner or later in life everything turns into work. Including work. I would like to have seen you.

**Theodore** Too late.

**Dorothy** Oh, Teddy. I was hoping you were a solution.

**Theodore** What to?

**Dorothy** A problem I have. Dorothy's deliverance.
Do you make lots of these films?

**Theodore** Three or four a year.

**Dorothy** I have a silly idea. Why not make them all here?
We've got enough beds.

**Theodore** It's a thought.
But what would your sister say?

**Dorothy** She'd be outraged. One reason why I asked.

**Theodore** So it's not a violation?

**Dorothy** Oh it is. It is. A violation. A pollution. A
desecration. Which is exactly what I want.
How can a body like the National Trust . . . so decent,
so worthy, so . . . dull . . . take over a house that has been
so grossly defiled?
A porn studio? The idea!
That's what I thought anyway.

**Theodore** These days? No. Who cares?

**Dorothy** Dorothy behind the times again.

*She laughs.*

You were going to be my security of tenure. And besides,
it might have been fun.

**Theodore** Porn isn't fun.

**Dorothy** The people are. You are.

**Theodore** It wouldn't work.
I said I could pay you £5,000.
I don't have it.

**Dorothy** I never for a moment thought you did.

Though you did mend the central heating. How much do plumbers cost?

**Theodore** About that. It's too late.

**Dorothy** Too late the golf club, too late the health farm, too late the adult entertainment. It won't be on in cinemas?

**Theodore** I wish.

**Dorothy** You wish what? Oh, it's another of those phrases. I'll never catch up . . . though at least I'm trying.
Will you send me it?

**Theodore** On DVD?

**Dorothy** Is that what it's called?

**Theodore** Do you have a player?

**Dorothy** No, but the vicar has one. I'd like to see the snaps too when you've got them developed.

**Theodore** I can show you now.

**Dorothy** Really? We used to have to go to the chemist in Mexborough.
Dear Mr Theodore. You made me remember how I used to like work . . . not work itself so much as the things to do with work . . . people fussing round, putting their hearts into it. In those days you see I didn't mind people. People were work.

**Theodore** And love.

*Dorothy nods.*

**Dorothy** Loving was never the problem. It was being loved I found hard to learn. Did you ever marry?

**Theodore** Sort of.

*Pause.*

Smile.

**Dorothy** I don't much feel like it.

**Theodore** Smile.

*She smiles, brilliantly.*

That's what I remember.

**Dorothy** I'd outlaw 'remember'. May I give you a kiss, still?

*She kisses him.*

And kiss Mr Grip. So tidy.
Teddy.
I know you won't come back.
But you can.

*She smiles again, but it is not the same.*
*He goes, as Louise runs on.*

**Louise** I just wanted to say goodbye. And this is moisturiser. This is proper shampoo. This is conditioner. And this is deodorant. Give it to Iris.

**Dorothy** Treats.

**Louise** Promise me you'll use them.

*She hugs Louise. They go. Stage empty.*
*Theodore and June come on.*

**June** I wouldn't come back if I were you.

**Theodore** I wasn't planning on it.

**June** I'm an archdeacon. I'm on excellent terms with the police. In fact it was a toss-up whether I went into the church or law enforcement. It would be most unwise.

*Dorothy (still in her couture) returns.*

Who were they?

**Dorothy** Just a film crew. They really liked the house. Said it was ideal.

**June** For a pornographic film, yes, I'm sure it was. Did you realise what they were doing?

**Dorothy** Me? I'm a recluse.

**Iris** I did. It was a mucky film. Some of them had their clothes off and they weren't even Canadian.

**Dorothy** The lovely thing was it was warm. You could sit on the pipes.

**June** Filth.

**Dorothy** Not filth. Adult.

**June** When we call things adult it's because we know they are childish.

**Dorothy** Is that from a sermon?

*The bell rings.*

This will be the man in the camel-hair coat. He said he would come back.

**June** What for?

**Dorothy** To clinch the deal, I imagine.

**June** He's going to get a surprise. Well, aren't you going to tell him to go round the back?

**Dorothy** No need. The front door works perfectly. Mr Grip again.

*She goes, leaving June and Iris alone.*

**Iris** She had a nice time. For a change. And the food was lovely. I've still got some somewhere. She had all her clothes out. Looked a picture.
And brown sauce.

**June** What?

**Iris** With the chips.

They lifted me up in my chair and carried me round the room. Normal people. You forget.

How's Guthrie?

Been to the North Pole yet?

*Bevan comes in with Dorothy.*

**Dorothy** Come in, come in.

**Bevan** I love this – Cardin?

**Dorothy** Hardy Amies.

**Bevan** And you, you're more . . .

**Dorothy** Normal?

**Bevan** Quite . . . Oh, company!

**Dorothy** My sister, I'm afraid. She's a clergyman.

**Bevan** So I see. I'm . . . the valuer.

**June** I know who you are. I gather you have a proposition. The attic sale?

**Bevan** Indeed. (*He fishes in his bag for the schedule.*) I have the schedule.

*He is handing it to Dorothy but June intercepts it.*

I should point out the estimates are very conservative. These days to tempt out the buyers we tend to lower prices on things.

**June** So I see.

However, happily I've no need to look at this. The contents, attics or anywhere else, are not for sale.

**Bevan** One was told they were.

**June** One was misinformed.

**Dorothy** My sister has other plans. She favours the National Trust.

**Bevan**  And, as I seem to remember, you don't?

**Dorothy**  One is still open to offers. Of which yours is the most tempting.

**Bevan**  The sale?

**Dorothy**  No. Your other hat.

*He says nothing.*

**June**  What other hat?

**Dorothy**  You can speak freely, it will go no further. My sister is discretion itself.

**Bevan**  Of course. I explained to your sister that though I came originally in connection with the attic sale . . .

**June**  Which is not going to happen.

**Bevan**  I also represent a group of entirely disinterested individuals who are putting together a portfolio of properties . . . call it 'The Best of Britain'.

**June**  And you want to buy this house?

**Bevan**  Provided it can be shifted from its situation in this somewhat truculent countryside – to Devon, say or Dorset – yes, we were very keen.

**Dorothy**  Were? Were? Do you not want it now?

**Bevan**  Oh yes. Desperately. But I'm afraid, dear lady, it could now be down the road a year or two.

**Dorothy**  'Down the road'?

**Bevan**  A postponement only. We have had a hiccup, some local silliness in the Middle East and our old friend the price of oil. Temporary though it is, it means that if the Trust is definite in its intentions we would not stand in its way. We have no objections to the Trust . . . we just come at the problem from another angle. It's a difference in detail. The Trust wants to get people in, we want to keep them out. Either way the house is preserved.

**June** Well, that resolves our dilemma. The house must go to the Trust.

**Dorothy** One question. Suppose we have something of extraordinary value which were we to sell I could go on living here on the proceeds?

**Bevan** The Adam rooms, you mean? In the thirties you could have stripped them out and sold them, but not nowadays. They're integral to the house.

**Dorothy** I wasn't thinking of them.

**June** We've been through this?

**Dorothy** Tell her.

**Bevan** I'm sorry?

**Dorothy** Iris.

*Iris gets something wrapped in newspaper out of the cupboard.*

The cat's bowl.

**June** The cat's bowl?

**Dorothy** When you came before you said this was Chinese and worth the house and its contents put together.

**Bevan** Oh dear, did I say that? I suppose I did. I remember now, it was just as I was going. Forgive me, but it's just a trick of the trade. When you're bidding for a sale as I was – and still am – you hit on some inoffensive object and bestow on it an inflated value . . . it's known as sale bait.

**Dorothy** So it's not Chinese? Not priceless?

**Iris** So what is it?

**Bevan**  Well, it's the cat's bowl. And very nice too . . . but not . . .

**June**  The solution to all our problems.

**Bevan**  And there is nothing else? Nothing one hasn't seen?

*Dorothy's fingers stray to her (hidden) necklace but she says nothing and nor does Iris.*
  *She sits.*

**Dorothy**  I thought I had a card up my sleeve.

**June**  I'm sorry we've wasted your time. And obviously, as I now confidently expect the house goes to the Trust, an attic sale is out of the question.

**Bevan**  Yes. I can see that and, as I say, had it been a couple of years hence it would have been different, but at the moment and unusually for us . . . all this hooliganism in the Middle East means that, multis though we are . . . we do have a cash flow problem. Besides which . . . there's no harm in saying this, we're in the process of acquiring a cathedral.

**June**  A cathedral?

**Dorothy**  A *cathedral*? But that's unthinkable.

**Bevan**  Precisely. But, we think the unthinkable. It was going to be Ripon, which is rather basic as cathedrals go, and as a building it's not well presented. But it would have been cheap and the diocese was happy to make it redundant. But instead we raised our sights somewhat and went for the big one.

**June**  Don't tell me. Winchester.

**Bevan**  You know?

**June**  I'm treasurer of the Inter-Diocesan Fabric Fund, of course I know. And I know you. You're Bevan of The Concern.

**Bevan**  And you're Huddersfield.

64

*They shake hands cordially.*

**June** The felicities of email!

I know it's pricey, but Winchester is such a good idea.

**Bevan** Isn't it? And after all, the school is private so why shouldn't the cathedral be private too?

**June** Quite. And since we shall be ploughing back most of the proceeds into pastoral work in the inner cities, who can object? The Archbishop can't wait.

Oh, I'm so pleased to have met you. No regrets about the house?

**Bevan** None. I shall look forward to coming round and seeing the place under its new dispensation.

*He shakes hands with Dorothy but Iris will have none of it.*

**June** (*as they are leaving*) Incidentally, I'd like to run past you a notion I've had for a series of exclusive celebrity eucharists, leading figures in business, sport and the world of entertainment.

**Bevan** Interesting!

**June** The service – I think I could get one of the archbishops, followed by a working breakfast . . .

**Bevan** The host on toast!

**June** Humour! Good solvent! Exchange of ideas . . .

**Bevan** We must do lunch . . .

*Dorothy ceremonially returns the cat's bowl to the floor again. Dorothy and Iris sing 'Walkin' Back to Happiness' but sadly.*
*June returns.*
*A pause.*

**Dorothy** I wish now I'd not caught up. You're all the same.

**June** Money talks to money. Always has, nothing new there. And be honest, aren't you longing to see it done up?

**Dorothy** I want it the way it's always been . . . not done up, not run down . . . just taken for granted. When did that stop?

**June** What?

**Dorothy** Taking things for granted.

**June** Where did you say you'd got to with the papers?

**Dorothy** The 1980s.

**June** About then. That was when the mine went.

**Dorothy** I took that for granted.

**June** So did they . . . along with a lot besides. Things changed. If it was worthwhile it had to be paid for. Everything had a price. If it didn't have a price it didn't have a value.
Oh, Dotty. What do you want?
You don't want the Trust. You don't want the damp. You don't want the people. What do you want?

**Dorothy** I long for the decay of England. Then at least we could stop blustering. England at a standstill and this just another stately home . . . not evaluated, not made special. Ordinary.

**June** Ordinary? This?

**Dorothy** Taken for granted. Is there a name for that? Is it a creed?

**June** Taking things for granted? It used to be called English but not any more.

**Dorothy** No. What they get now is a version of England.
'Our houses,' they think as they trail round.
'Our land.'

Only it isn't – and it never was.
It's just their ration.
England – serving suggestion.
These people who'll come round – will they be Brits?

**June** Mostly.

**Dorothy** Who are Brits?

**June** Today's people.

**Dorothy** When did they come in?

**June** (*fading*) The eighties again.

*The house is newly transformed, part of which may
be a vision of the Adam saloon at the rear of the stage,
an almost celestial vision in green and yellow. The
transformation should be spectacular.*
    *Through all this Ralph Lumsden is much in evidence.
Dorothy draws him aside.*

**Dorothy** Mr Lumsden. There's something I should have
told you. My sister won't have mentioned it.

**Lumsden** Lady Dorothy.

**Dorothy** We've just had a film company here. When the
house was already on offer to the Trust.

**Lumsden** No problem there. The Trust often plays host
to movies. It's a valuable source of income.

**Dorothy** This was different. It was what I can only
describe as a dirty movie.

**Lumsden** How dirty?

**Dorothy** Very.

**Lumsden** Really. Can we access it? Because I'm sure the
house will have seen worse.

*She acknowledges defeat and is going.*

You see, Lady Dorothy. There is no pollution that time does not expunge, no affront that indifference will not embrace. You wouldn't like me to call a halt?

**Dorothy** No. Bring it on.

*The transformation scene concluded, June and Dorothy address the audience.*

**June** I am relieved. The house has come home and my spirits rise.

**Dorothy** No one hands over their house without some sense of throwing in the towel. My spirits fall.

**June** As a priest I am happy for the Trust to be the beneficiary.

**Dorothy** Of course you are. The Trust is a church, too, and in the piety and devotion of its members one that would rival the Anglicans were their membership not virtually the same. The cars boast their pilgrim badge, the stickers the holy houses where they have paid homage and the sacrament they have received of coffee and walnut cake.

**June** This is the zeal of thine house.

**Lumsden** (*this too is partly to the audience*) What I always feel is that every one of our houses has a story to tell. Once upon a time the thinking was that this just meant the posh parts . . . the state rooms, the formal gardens. Then we started to open up the kitchens and the below stairs. But still it was a tidy, manicured version of the life lived here and visitors always wanted more. Or different. With this house we are trying to tell it like it is. Take the old newspapers . . .

**Dorothy** They've gone.

**Lumsden** I know. Tidied away, the newspapers burned.

**Dorothy** That was Bruce, the grip. A lovely man but with the soul of a housemaid.

**Lumsden** Ashes in the boiler room. So sad.

**Dorothy** We were warm at least.

**Lumsden** A more grievous loss is the collection – the anthology one might almost say – of chamber pots. Oh, they're still there, washed and gleaming, it's true, but now voided of their contents . . . the urine of Kipling, Belloc, Elgar and Shaw flushed wantonly down the promiscuous loo.

**Dorothy** (*shaking her head*) Bruce again.

**Lumsden** Which is a particular sadness to me as it was this ancient wee that gave me the clue how to tell the tale of this unique house.

But take heart. All is not lost. By a process the scrupulous might call dishonest but I prefer to call cosmetic the ancient newspapers have been replaced and even as we speak the chamber pots are being replenished.

*Perhaps we should see someone taking away one of the pots as someone else brings back another that has been refilled.*

Thanks here are due to the valiant efforts of our devoted staff and with none but the purist (and a purist equipped to test DNA) any the wiser.

In the meantime we have a problem.

**June** You.

**Lumsden** What are we going to do with you?

**June** You don't want to sit in your room all day, even with an en-suite bathroom.

**Dorothy** I could live in the lodge.

**Lumsden** That would be a pity, I think, hinting at dispossession. Besides, I need you to round off the story of the house. The Stacpoole Experience . . . One would prefer you to preside . . . even to pass through.

**Dorothy** A living ghost.

**Lumsden** No.

**Dorothy** An object of pity.

**Lumsden** An object of interest.

**Dorothy** But an object. I was an object as a model and now once again.

**Lumsden** Everything here is an object.

**Dorothy** I have ended up like the house, pretending to be myself.

**June** There's no need to be nice to the visitors, or even talk to them if you don't want.

**Lumsden** It would be work.

**June** And you were saying how you'd forgotten you liked work.

**Iris** If it's work does she get paid?

**Lumsden** The Trust tends to regard work as voluntary.
   Going on from there . . . and you must forgive me for asking . . . but are you wedded to couture? You see, the story we are trying to tell . . . call it the rise and fall of a great house . . . would, I feel, climax better with you as I first saw you so memorably kitted out in fur coat and gym shoes.

**Dorothy** So I should change?

**June** Dotty. You might even enjoy it.

**Dorothy** Never. (*She goes.*) I'll change.

*Leaving Lumsden, June and Iris.*
  *The coal cracks.*

**Lumsden** Of course, it could all . . . fall through.

**June** What?

**Lumsden** You've been very naughty, Archdeacon, very naughty indeed.
  The coal?

**June** I didn't want to put you off.

**Lumsden** The whole place could be on the verge of collapse.

**June** No, I promise you . . .

**Lumsden** Naughty.
  One cannot ignore it so I've had the experts round and they assure me that despite these subterranean grumblings the place is quite sound.

**Iris** I could have told you that.

**June** Forgive me.

**Lumsden** But that sound! One feels on board a ship about to hit the rocks. It seems a shame to deny our visitors a similar thrill, so the upshot is I'm having the sound recorded and we will play it at random intervals during opening hours.
  Which leaves just you, Iris.

**Iris** Me?

**Lumsden** You are a bit of a loose end.

**Iris** But I've spent my life here. I am as much part of the story as they are.

**Lumsden** I'm sure . . .

**Iris** And I am not a loose end. I am . . .

**June**  Yes, we know. The companion.

**Iris**  No. I am not the companion.
I am the sister.

**June**  Half. The half-sister. There's no need for you to know this.

**Lumsden**  Please. I'm fascinated.

**Iris**  My mother was from the village, over at the colliery. She was a maid here. Their father, the lord, was my father. I am older than both of you. And I would never have given it to the Trust. I'd have made a go of it.

**Lumsden**  But this is perfect.

**June**  It mustn't ever be said.

**Iris**  Why not? I don't mind.

**Lumsden**  And it all fits.
Can I let you in on my long-term thinking *vis à vis* the house? Do you see the row of colliery dwellings on the crest of the hill?

**June**  You can't see them. That's why the trees are there.

**Lumsden**  Exactly. Clumped there by your father, lest they offend the eye, though they were his cottages and his mine. The Trust's plan is to fell the trees so that the house will have an uninterrupted view of the cottages, and the cottages of the house, and visitors to the one could stroll across the valley to see the other. The house-to-house walk. And with both open to view, at one stroke, visitors all, class and privilege are abolished. And here is Iris, the living link between the two. And if she occasionally lets slip that all this could have been hers, visitors will come away enchanted.

**Iris**  They'll think I'm mad.

**Lumsden**  Better still!

**Iris** And will you tell the story of the colliery disaster?

**Lumsden** I want to tell it all. Shabby and disreputable though the house has become, tell its story candidly and people will come.

**Iris** And however personal? That too?
    Because my sister, as I am now permitted to call her, had a miscarriage . . .

*Dorothy comes in.*

**Dorothy** Oh, tell him, Iris. Tell him it all. My unled life. Show him the attic. Show him the chest of drawers. You could even mock up the parcel. The baby.

**Iris** Yes, it's upstairs somewhere.

**Lumsden** Heartrending though these revelations are, I would be failing in my duty if I did not try and incorporate them into the story of the house. Because that is what visitors want. And ultimately, you see, there is nothing that cannot be said, nowhere that is not visitable. That at least the Holocaust has taught us.

*Possibly half of what follows is recorded and done as if through headphones.*
    *A group comes round, including June. Visitors blunder around, half of them with headphones on, others watching a screen.*

**Dorothy** (*now in fur coat and plimsolls*) The chimney piece is rather fun. It's one of several in the house by a designer called William Kent. You will see that some of Kent's classical motifs have been supplemented by some vernacular additions, the work of Canadian troops stationed here just before D-Day. No attempt has been made to repair or disguise these graffiti on the principle that they too have their own posterity. Elsewhere in the house you will have seen more decorous graffiti done by

73

some of Cromwell's soldiers billeted here during the Civil War. Those we cherish as one day we will cherish these more lively and crudely illustrative carvings. And so they troop about on their disconsolate patrol.

*June claps her.*

Somebody tipped me the other day. I said, 'That's awfully sweet of you,' and gave it to Iris. That's what the Queen does, isn't it? . . . Gives it to the lady in waiting.

**Iris** It was only 50p.

*She goes.*

**Dorothy** Maybe you shouldn't see this last bit.

**June** (*looking at the screen*) It's only your costumes. Oh, and Dad's Coronation robes. Were they in the attic too?

**Dorothy** This is the bit.
Lumsden insisted it should go in. He says it's the future. This is my scene.

**June** Oh, Dottie.

**Dorothy** I don't mind.
This bit's on what's called a loop . . . we've seen that bottom before, you see . . . here it comes again.
She was from Latvia.
You can freeze-frame if you want to.
I understand all this now. It's what they call interactive. It's fun.

**June** Oh, darling. I'm sorry.

**Lumsden** Sorry? What for?
We love her.
She's made such a *journey*.
Epic. She's our woman of the year.

*He goes.*

**Dorothy** If I'm on the door when they're going I'll sometimes say, 'And did you find what you were looking for?'

They never know, of course.

I could tell them.

A comforting parable, a life like mine. An antidote to envy. Celebrity, aristocracy, the lofty brought low.

So they'll go out reassured as, say, the life of Judy Garland reassures them. Or the death of Diana.

Life is fair after all, that is the message. Only sometimes they look at me like this and say, 'Poor you. How sad.'

And do you know what I say? I say, 'Get over it.'

*June kisses and hugs her. Dorothy is unmoved.*

I hate it. Still, it's been a life.

*The last person waiting to leave is Louise from the film unit.*

**Dorothy** Louise!

**Louise** Look at you. Oh, Dorothy, what happened to your lovely dress?

**Dorothy** This is my costume now. Are you by yourself?

**Louise** Today – but he is coming.

**Dorothy** Don't go there.

**Louise** You could always email him.

**Dorothy** That's true. Email. Facebook. No one is ever far away.

*They laugh.*

I *know*.

**Louise** Still got your beads.

*Dorothy fingers the rosary round her neck. She kisses Louise, who is going.*

**Dorothy**  Yes. Wait.

*She takes the rosary off and gives it to her.*

**Louise**  No, no.

**Dorothy**  They're only beads, after all. Fashion, like everything else.

*She fastens them for her. Louise goes.*

Lost let lost be and not found.
Gone should gone be and not fetched back.

*She activates the announcement then she slowly turns each section of the lights off with her iPod.*

**A Recorded Voice**  'The House is now closed.
The House is now closed.'

*A pause. The coal cracks.
Lights fade.*

*The End.*